Advance Praise for *The Empowered Citizens Guide*

"These are very practical and tangible steps—not esoteric sermons of high-minded values or calls to 'get involved.' It helps answer the question 'What do I do today to move this forward?'"

Joe Kriesberg, *Massachusetts Association of Community Development Corporations*

"The writing style is engaging, the approach is hands-on and practical, and the text puts the reader in the moment where things are happening. The timing is impeccable. This book makes you feel that you can actually reach out and do this."

John McNutt, *University of Delaware*

"Pat Libby is well-known and regarded as an expert in this field. This book is excellent and achieves what it sets out to do: create a user-friendly guide for laypeople on how to engage in lobbying."

Shannon Williams, *Alliance for Justice*

"Crisp and concise."

Peter Rose, *Sard Verbinnen & Co.*

"*The Empowered Citizens Guide* does a fantastic job demystifying the political process and invites average citizens into policymaking in a way that feels both empowering and doable."

D'Arlyn Bell, *University of Kansas/Cherokee Nation*

"The 10-step process is logical, easy to follow, and can be a useful reference in visualizing and walking through key elements of a successful campaign."

Steven Eldred, *The California Endowment*

T0346927

THE EMPOWERED CITIZENS GUIDE

THE EMPOWERED CITIZENS GUIDE

10 Steps to Passing a Law that Matters to You

Pat Libby

OXFORD
UNIVERSITY PRESS

Oxford University Press is a department of the University of Oxford.
It furthers the University's objective of excellence in research, scholarship,
and education by publishing worldwide. Oxford is a registered trade mark of
Oxford University Press in the UK and certain other countries.

Published in the United States of America by Oxford University Press
198 Madison Avenue, New York, NY 10016, United States of America.

Library of Congress Cataloging-in-Publication Data
Names: Libby, Pat, author.
Title: The empowered citizens guide : 10 steps to passing a law that
matters to you / Pat Libby.
Description: New York : Oxford University Press, 2022. |
Includes bibliographical references. | Summary: "This book is intended for
foundation leaders, nonprofit and social service professionals,
committed nonprofit agency volunteers, members of neighborhood
associations, and members of the general public who want to understand
how to pass a law"— Provided by publisher.
Identifiers: LCCN 2021039960 | ISBN 9780197601631 (paperback) |
ISBN 9780197601648 (pdf) | ISBN 9780197601655 (epub) | ISBN 9780197601662
Subjects: LCSH: Legislation—United States—Citizen participation. |
LCGFT: Law for laypersons.
Classification: LCC KF4945 .L53 2022 | DDC 328.73/077—dc23
LC record available at https://lccn.loc.gov/2021039960

1 3 5 7 9 8 6 4 2

Printed and bound by Sheridan Books, Inc., United States of America

CONTENTS

CONTENTS

PREFACE

For years, I saw lawmaking as a spectator sport. I didn't know anything about the process until I found myself in a job where I had to learn how to lobby to get laws passed. Turns out, I was pretty good at it.

Years later, I landed in a different job where I taught everyday citizens how to pass laws. Most of them knew nothing when they got started. Yet many of those folks surprised themselves by passing a law on their first try. I taught them by breaking down the process from start to finish into 10 easy-to-follow steps. Now, I've written this book to share the 10 Steps with you.

This book is for anyone—from newbie to been-there-and-failed—who wants to understand how to successfully put together a lobbying campaign.

If you are passionate about creating change in your community, city, or state, read more for a simple recipe that you can use to make a difference.

ACKNOWLEDGMENTS

I have loved writing this book. I've loved it because so many people have given so generously of themselves in the process.

Annamarie Maricle and Travis Degheri are at the top of the list. Annamarie summoned the courage to tell you her very personal story because she was motivated to help other moms learn how to make real change through the legislative process. Travis, one of her lobbying campaign partners, was equally passionate about sharing his experience with you. Their story is a central part of this book, and is critically important to making the 10 Steps come alive.

A host of other people took the time to carefully review the book's chapters. They provided kind and concrete feedback that allowed me to include some items I'd forgotten or glossed over. The book would have been okay without their input, but it's that much better because of it. Some of these folks I knew well; others, I had never met. Yet all took the time to carefully review and think about the book. A few of my friends (indicated with an asterisk) did double duty by reading another book I had written on this topic, which allowed them to offer especially insightful comments on this one.

This wonderful group of reviewers included:

- D'Arlyn Bell, *University of Kansas*
- Tabitha Bonilla, *Northwestern University*
- Steven Eldred, *The California Endowment*
- Elizabeth Heagy, *Heagy Nonprofit Consulting Services LLC*
- Richard Hoefer, *University of Texas at Arlington**
- Joe Kriesberg, *Massachusetts Association of Community Development Corporations**
- Abby Levine, *Alliance for Justice**
- John McNutt, *University of Delaware**
- Peter Rose, *Sard Verbinnen & Co.*
- Patrice Sulton, *DC Justice Lab*
- Lori Thiel, *League of Women Voters, San Diego*
- L. Joy Williams, *Brooklyn NAACP*
- Shannon Williams, *Alliance for Justice**

Alyssa Palazzo, my dog-loving editor, has been a champion of this book from the very beginning. In fact, I can't remember which one of us dreamed up the idea of my writing it. During the review process, she wrote comments in the margins at the points where she laughed out loud. She refrained from scolding me too much about run-on sentences (I also learned she frowns on parenthesis). Matthew Dix cheerfully assisted both of us with incredible attention to detail, patience, and unfailing good humor.

Miles, my dog, provided inspiration for several passages in the book. He also made sure that I took him for an afternoon walk when I needed to step away from my computer. This assured he got an extra treat as well, so it was a fair deal all around.

Finally, and most importantly, I am grateful every day for the loving support of my husband, Mike Eichler. He's my best friend, personal chef, sounding board, cheerleader (sans polyester shorts), and co-conspirator. Our love affair began decades ago with a series of endless long-distance phone calls. We haven't stopped talking and loving each other since.

CONTRIBUTORS

Travis Degheri, PhD, is a leadership consultant, researcher, and change facilitator. He resides in Portland, Oregon, with his wife and three children.

Annamarie Maricle has worked as a professional fundraiser and grant writer for more than 20 years. She lives in San Diego, California.

Introduction

Why this Book was Written for You

THE STORY BEHIND THE 10 STEPS

This book is for you and for people like you who aren't afraid of what they don't know.

It was written for you, a citizen of this fine country (or, perhaps, an aspiring citizen) on the assumption that you don't know much, or as much as you'd like, about how laws are made or how public policy is shaped.

It was written for you if you're feeling mad as hell about something that's been going on in your community, city, or state and find yourself muttering over and over "There ought to be a law!"

It was written for you if you're an average Joe, Janette, or none of the above, part of a grassroots group or a block club, work or volunteer for a nonprofit, or are a member of a coalition.

It was written for you if you've tried talking to politicians about a change you think needs to happen, haven't made a whole lot of progress or as much progress as you'd like, and are looking for some insight on how to get a law passed.

It was written for you if you believe in your heart that even though the odds may to be stacked against you, you can stand up to the big boys and pass a law without breaking your piggy bank.

This book is for you regardless of whether you are brand new to this whole concept or have already waded into the advocacy ocean and want to learn new strategies that will enable you to be more effective.

It is for you if you're willing to roll up your sleeves, figure out what it's all about, and use your newly acquired skills to create positive change. Congratulations on buying this book, which is the first step in that process.

Before you continue reading, I want to let you in on a little secret: You don't have to understand all the intricacies of the legislative process to pass a law, just like you don't have to be a veterinarian to own a dog. In fact, you probably already have what you need: passion for your cause and some good, hard facts about "it"—the "it" being the thing that needs to be funded or changed to make life better. Our elected officials, wise as many are, don't know everything there is to know about everything. That is why they rely on *you*, a real person who is living in the real world, to educate them about issues that are important. It's that simple.

The goal of this book is to empower you to create the change you want to see happen. The heart of it is a 10-step strategy—the 10 Steps— for passing laws. The strategy has been used by many people to get some important laws on the books at the state and local level.

A volunteer and her friends followed the 10 Steps to pass a state law requiring Little League coaches to undergo background checks for child abuse and financial crimes; nonprofit staffers used the steps to pass a state law mandating that computer repair techs report child pornography to the police; another group went step by step to pass a law requiring pets to be included in domestic violence restraining orders; a student group followed the steps to extend housing subsidies in California for foster youth until age 26 (it had been 18); an environmental group used the 10 Steps to pass a law mandating the state clean up pollution along the US-Mexico border; elderly advocates did the 10-Step tango to strengthen protections for nursing home residents by requiring greater penalties for abuse infractions and mandating greater liability insurance. The list goes on and on. To top it off, most of these folks had *never* talked to a lawmaker before they learned the 10 Steps!

To help you see it clear as day, this book will walk you step by step through the story of how a mother, whose son's addiction was fueled by over-the-counter drugs, fought alongside a few friends to pass a law that addressed a root cause of the problem.

Of course, I can't claim that you'll automatically succeed in passing a law if you use the 10 Steps. There are always exceptions to the rule—like common-sense gun laws that, for maddening reasons which defy logic, meet incredible amounts of resistance. And even if you have a home run of an idea that everyone seems to agree on, you'll still be competing for the time and attention of legislators who are hearing from other people who have all sorts of other worthwhile ideas that may beat out yours. Sometimes you have to keep at it for a few years before you hit pay dirt. As my friend Joe[1] says, "The legislative process is designed to be hard. It should be hard. There should be a high bar before the government uses its power to take money (taxes), spend money, or impose restrictions on our freedom." Still, if you don't play, you can't win, and the more you work at it, the more likely you are to have success.

I pieced together the 10 Steps when I was hired to run a nonprofit where a big part of my job was lobbying. If you gasped when you read the word *lobbying*, take a deep breath—all it means is working to influence lawmakers. When I started that job, I was conscientious about voting in every election, gave a little money to

---

1. Thanks for these pearls of wisdom, Joe Kriesberg. Joe is a dear friend, brilliant attorney, professor, and community activist from Boston.

a few candidates, posted some campaign signs in my front window, and considered myself to be a well-informed citizen. But I had *no* idea what lobbying was all about or how the legislative process worked (and I mean zero, zip, nada, none). So, I did what any red-blooded American would do: I made it up as I went along! Much to my amazement, I discovered that I was actually good at lobbying.

Several years later, I became a professor who taught students how to use my 10-step model, and sure enough, *they* had success passing laws. That experience made me think about how powerful it would be if *anyone* who wanted to pass a law knew these simple steps. That's why I wrote this book.

I can't remember being taught civics in high school, or maybe I nodded off that day because Mr. Wright (may he rest in peace) was a pretty boring teacher and my assigned seat was in the back row, where I had to squint to see the blackboard. In any case, I'm going to assume that your starting point for learning this stuff was the same as mine and the students I taught—zero. In fact, it doesn't matter if you've never stepped foot inside your city hall, county building, or state capitol and the closest you've gotten to an elected official is waving at a parade float. This book will provide you with:

- An explanation of terms related to advocacy and lobbying.
- A detailed overview of the 10 Steps, with each one illustrated by a real-life example of how it was used to build a successful lobbying campaign.
- For those of you who volunteer for or work at a nonprofit, an easy-to-follow explanation of the legal rules for public charities that want to lobby.

The best way to learn is by doing. This book is designed to guide you through the process as you are engaged in the act of creating your lobbying campaign. Please write to tell me which parts of the book were particularly helpful to you and which could have been clearer. That way, others can learn from *you*. And if you're willing to share the details of your experience, we might even share your story with future readers!

Chapter 1

A Quick Roadmap to the Lawmaking Process

Lawmaking is a lot like sports.

I don't mean that it's a game with winners and losers, although it can sometimes feel that way; I mean that it has its own special rules and language. Think about it: Folks who don't follow basketball don't know what a three-second violation is; a baseball fan might stare blankly at a soccer fan talking about an offside, while the soccer fan shrugs at a story about a squeeze play. I'll be darned if I have a clue about what a pulling guard does in a football game. Pretty much every field of work—whether sports, plumbing, massage, landscaping, what have you—has its own unique terminology and ways of doing things that aren't familiar to people who don't do that type of work. The legislative process is no different, except that what lawmakers do affects everyone who lives in this country.

Since many of us were more focused on our raging hormones than on high school civics, I'll start with the basics of what we think we should know but don't (or forgot) about how a bill becomes a law, the difference between lobbying and advocacy, how the playing field is laid out, and who the players are.

FOLLOWING THE YELLOW BRICK ROAD

Legislation starts with a certain set of ideas that are developed by lawmakers or advocates—the advocates being people like you who have an idea about something that needs to be changed. Often, advocates start with a big idea that will morph as it goes through the policy-making process. During that time, other legislators and the public (including other lobbyists, organizations, and regular citizens) will have an opportunity to express their views on what is being proposed.

As a result, the lawmaking process is difficult. It's designed to be difficult so that the end product—the law that results—reflects the best thinking about a particular idea. It involves a lot of cooks stirring the broth and adding a pinch here and there (otherwise known as input, compromise, and negotiation) because, at the end of the day, the legislature is deciding how it's going to use its power and (our) money to affect the lives of the people it serves.

Just like Dorothy in *The Wizard of Oz*, there is a winding path that advocates need to follow on the way to getting a law passed. In its most basic form (and really, this is all you need to know) on the *state* and *federal* levels, it looks like this:

- A bill starts in one house when a legislator who *authors* a bill *introduces* it. That bill is given a number, which allows everyone who is interested in it to track its progress.
- The bill is then brought to a committee that oversees a particular at subject area, where a *hearing* takes place. During that hearing, people can voice their opinions on the bill (those people being advocates, lobbyists, and committee members).
- Ideally, the committee approves it. This is referred to as having the bill *pass out of committee.*
- If it doesn't have to go to a different committee[1] for a similar hearing, the bill goes to the *floor* of that house so that all the members of that chamber can vote on it.

---

1. For instance, my friend Howard Wayne, a former California assemblyman, authored a statewide bill having to do with testing ocean water that had to go through both a Local Government Committee and an Environmental Safety Committee. Often, things that cost a lot of money will have to go through a fiscal committee, such as an Appropriations Committee.

- Assuming the bill passes the house of origin, it then goes through the same process in the other side (also known as the other house) and, ideally, passes.

Not surprisingly, things can get bogged down at different stages in the process. For instance, the bill may not be voted out of committee and may *die*. It could pass one house and be squashed in the other. Or the bill's language (and intent) could change when it goes to the other chamber. If that happens, the bill can still survive, but it needs to go back to the first house to be voted on again. In other words, *a bill must pass each house with the exact same language for it to become law.* Sometimes a conference committee, consisting of members of both houses, meets to iron out an agreement on the bill's language to make that happen.

When all is said and done, the president or governor signs or vetoes the bill. If the chief elected official vetoes it, legislators can vote on it again and can pass the bill if they have enough support to *override* the veto.

Your job as an advocate is to insert yourself, along with the other people who are part of your lobbying campaign, into the middle of this process so that your voices are heard throughout.

The process is similar on the county, city, or other local level except, as you probably already know, with local government there is only one legislative chamber! Therefore, the "bill"[2] (in this case, called an ordinance, resolution, or measure) starts with the elected official who is proposing it, goes to a committee for a hearing, and is then voted on by the full body (for example, the entire city council) for (ideally) approval by a majority

---

2. To keep things simple, I'm going to keep using the word *bill* throughout the book to describe legislation that is proposed at any level of government, from state to local, even though it would probably be called an *ordinance, measure, resolution,* or something along those lines when it's being proposed by a legislator representing a county, city, or town.

vote.[3] Once it passes, the chief elected official (if there is one; some cities, for example, don't have a strong mayor form of government) gets to sign or veto the item.

BUT, in the case of a veto at the state or local level, if there aren't enough votes from the legislators to override it, citizens have one more option: They can put together a *ballot campaign* that will ask the public to vote to create that law. Once legislation becomes law, it is called an *act* or a *statute*.

On the federal level only, the president has the authority to issue *executive orders*, which in essence create temporary laws that circumvent the legislative process. That practice has been used more and more by recent presidents because—newsflash!—Congress has been so polarized it's made oil and water look like best friends. Ultimately, executive orders can be unraveled through legislation or through the actions of a new president.

To be fair, my short explanation of the lawmaking process is pretty much like describing the game of baseball like this: There is a field laid out in a diamond shape with a *base* on each point. Players from Team A stand on and around the bases. A player called a *pitcher* stands in the middle and throws a ball to a player from Team B who is standing at a base. That player tries to hit the ball with a specially shaped *bat*. The object is to hit the ball so that no one on the other team can catch it. Ideally, the player will hit the ball, touch all the bases, and score a *run*. The team *up at bat* has three tries to hit the ball before the other team has a chance. This goes on for nine *innings*. The team with the most runs wins!

Obviously, just like my explanation of baseball, the lawmaking process is more complicated than I described. However, just as you

---

3. Some places require a *supermajority* vote for a bill to pass. You need to look at the rules for your state and local government to understand exactly how the system works in your area.

could enjoy a baseball game on a beautiful summer day without knowing what a breaking ball is, you can pass a law without being an expert on the legislative process—especially if you follow the 10 Steps outlined in this book.

Having a roadmap to making law is a good start. Honestly, though, the most important thing for you to know as a citizen advocate and lobbyist are the facts about the issue you care about.[4] As you work on developing a lobbying campaign using the 10 Steps, your legislative allies will guide your journey by explaining what comes next and offer insights as you ride out the bumps along the road.

WHAT'S THE DIFFERENCE BETWEEN ADVOCACY AND LOBBYING?

Lobbying and advocacy are kissing cousins. Advocacy is the big tent that includes lobbying along with a whole bunch of other activities that are designed to bring attention to an idea—for instance, organizing a rally or raising awareness of the issue on social media, among other things. Lobbying is the slice of advocacy that mostly involves contacting legislators about a particular bill. My friends at Alliance for Justice[5] like to explain it this way: "All lobbying is advocacy, but not all advocacy is lobbying."

I love to use Mothers Against Drunk Driving (MADD) when I explain the difference between advocacy and lobbying. When MADD first developed and promoted the concept of a *designated*

---

4. And, if you work for a 501(c)(3) nonprofit, the legal rules for lobbying, which you can read about in the Appendix.
5. Alliance for Justice offers a whole slew of helpful tools and trainings. You can find them at https://bolderadvocacy.org/

driver, they had a huge influence on the public's thinking about driving drunk (it's hard to imagine anyone today who is clueless about what being a designated driver means—unless they are playing stupid on purpose). Putting that brilliant idea into people's heads was advocacy at its best.

In 2000, MADD took a giant step further when it successfully lobbied the federal government to adopt a blood alcohol level of 0.08 as the federal standard for drunk driving. That federal standard was then tied to the distribution of national highway funds to states. As a result, by 2004 all 50 states and the District of Columbia had passed 0.08 as the legal drunk driving limit! And MADD didn't stop there. As of 2019, it passed all-offender laws in 34 states mandating that drunk drivers with a 0.08 blood alcohol level receive an ignition interlock device for at least 30 days, regardless of whether or not it was their first offense.[i] Now that's an impressive result for a lobbying campaign!

SIMPLE STUFF THAT MIGHT NOT BE IN YOUR MEMORY BANK

I really hate it when someone assumes that I should know something just because they toss around a word or concept without a care. Do you mean to tell me that everyone knew what a *pandemic* was prior to a few years ago? Because of that, this part of the chapter will review some terms that you might think you should know but aren't really all that clear on. It reminds me of that great song by David Roth, "Don't Should on Me," where he sings "Don't should on me and I won't should on you."[6] In other words, there's no need

---

6. Hear the song at https://www.youtube.com/watch?v=euaUmI75KBM

to feel embarrassed because you haven't been crystal clear on some of these things before.

A *legislator* is any type of lawmaker, and a *legislature* is a body of lawmakers. *Congress* is the term we use for our national legislature. And just like Congress, all legislatures at the state level (with the exception of Nebraska[7]) are divided into two *houses*—each side is also referred to as a *chamber.* One side is the Senate, which is always the smaller house because it has fewer members. It is the more powerful of the two chambers because fewer *members* represent more people.

The house with the most members is called different things depending on which state you live in. It might be known as the House of Representatives (which is what it's also called on the federal level), the House of Delegates, or the Assembly. The members of those chambers are referred to as *representatives, delegates,* or *assembly members.* People who are registered to vote are eligible to vote for a senator and a House member to represent them at the state level and, on the federal level, can vote for two senators and a House member.

Some states have a full-time legislature that is supported by a professional staff. Many state legislatures meet only a few months each year; in a handful of cases, legislators meet only every other year. It's easy to look up your own state online to see how your legislature functions.[8]

Legislation is a proposed law that is under consideration by a governing body that can make laws. That governing body might be

---

7. Nebraska has what is called a *unicameral legislature,* which means that it only has one chamber.
8. If you really want to get your nerd on, you can go to website of the National Conference of State Legislatures (https://www.ncsl.org), where you can see their five-tier classification of state legislatures across the country, which is organized by whether they are full-time, in the middle, very part-time, or somewhere in between those categories.

the US Congress, a state legislature, a county government, a city council, or a small municipality like a town or village council.

According to the IRS, legislation also includes "action . . . with respect to acts, bills, resolutions, or similar items (such as legislative confirmation of appointive office)."[ii] You'll often hear legislation referred to as a *bill*; for example, "a bill has been proposed to make July 18th a state holiday called Pat Libby Day!" (my birthday, in case you were wondering).

Lobbying is "a specific, legally defined activity that involves stating your position on specific legislation to legislators and/or asking them to support your position."[iii] Let's break that down.

You are *lobbying* when you (or people you organize, officially called the *grassroots*) make a direct appeal to legislators (or someone who works in that person's office) to do something specific about a law or a proposed law. You're lobbying when you're trying to find a legislator who will *author* or *carry*[9] a bill that represents the ideas you and your allies want to advance. You're lobbying when you're trying to repeal a law that's been passed or to amend a law to make it better. You're lobbying when you're trying to get more money for an existing program. It doesn't matter if you or your allies are advocating for or against a particular piece of legislation; you are lobbying when you and other people you organize directly appeal to lawmakers to take action. That's what this book will teach you how to do.

Occasionally, the general public acts as the legislature when it establishes a law as a result of a ballot question, such as through an initiative petition, a referendum, or a proposed constitutional amendment. So, in the case of a ballot campaign, if you make a direct appeal to the public to vote one way or another, you're

9. These words mean the same thing.

lobbying. And if you vote on a ballot question, you are a member of a legislative body—how cool is that?!

Many people are surprised to learn that school boards and zoning boards aren't legislatures. Why? Because they can't make laws. Therefore, when you go to those groups (and others bodies like them, such as housing authorities, water and sewer districts, etc.) to express your views, you're not technically lobbying. That doesn't mean that you should ignore them, though, because they do shape public policy that can have an impact on the quality of your life and on others in your community.

THERE WON'T BE A POP QUIZ

When you are lobbying at the local, city, county, or state level, no one is going to quiz you about whether or not you know what the next steps are in the lawmaking process. More often, the policymakers with whom you'll work, and their aides (especially those aides— bless them!), will help you navigate your way through it. What they will insist you know is everything possible about the idea or cause you are championing. That is the single most important thing you need to do to be an effective lobbyist. Know your stuff, and know how to present it effectively.

Trust me, having a deep understanding of the issue that you're lobbying on is MUCH more important than having a PhD in government when it comes to passing a law! There is no substitute for lived experience.

Once you learn to lobby, you'll not only embrace it, you'll wonder how you ever got along without knowing how. Mostly, you'll be amazed at what you can get done!

REFERENCES

i. Mothers Against Drunk Driving. (2019). MADD Helps Pass Lifesaving Laws in 2019. Retrieved February 25, 2020, from https://www.madd.org/madd-rates-all-50-states-on-drunk-driving-laws
ii. Internal Revenue Service. (2021). *Lobbying*. Retrieved September 8, 2021, from https://www.irs.gov/charities-non-profits/lobbying
iii. Center for Lobbying in the Public Interest. (2006). *Make a Difference for Your Cause*. Retrieved September 8, 2021, from https://www.councilofnonprofits.org/sites/default/files/documents/Make_a_Difference_RG%5B1%5D.pdf

Chapter 2

Introducing the 10 Steps

The 10 Steps are a recipe for how to put together a lobbying campaign. Many people and organizations—most with little or no previous lobbying experience—have followed the steps one by one to construct successful campaigns that have resulted in important new laws. The steps have been helpful as well for organizations that have lobbied in the past and are looking for new strategies.

The formula for successful lobbying is a little bit like the secret ingredients that make Coke taste like Coke and not Pepsi—that is, they're completely mysterious to people who aren't on the inside. In this case, though, I want to share the recipe with anyone who is committed to making legislative change.

When I cook, I start by laying out all of the ingredients I need on the kitchen counter so that I can think about how everything will go together. That's why I want you to see a list of the 10 Steps before I go into a detailed explanation about each one. Some steps might seem obvious on the surface—how they're named should give you a big clue about what each particular step is all about—but the deeper you dig, the more you'll understand each one's importance and how it fits with the others.

1. Identify an issue. The issue you want to fix or get funding for is usually something that a whole bunch of people in your neighborhood, community group, or profession recognize is an issue, problem, or need. It sounds simple and obvious, but sometimes it's not.

2. Research the issue. Research involves searching for facts and figures from experts and reliable sources that back up your position (and I don't mean "alternative facts"!). In addition to formal research studies, "experts" should include people in your neighborhood or community, folks your nonprofit serves, or other people like you who have experienced something earthshattering or are excited by whatever it is you want to fix or change. You'll also want to find out whether anyone has passed a similar law in another place, and do some rough calculations about what your bill might cost to implement. I know it sounds complicated, but I'll break it down into bite sized pieces in Chapter 4.

3. Create a fact sheet. The name of this step is a little bit misleading because it actually involves creating two documents—a position paper that summarizes your research *and* a fact sheet.

Once you have done a deep dive into researching your issue, you'll put the highlights into a *white paper* (otherwise called a *position paper/case statement/policy paper*—take your pick and call it what you want) that lays out your case. The white paper will explain why this issue is important, why the change you propose is needed, and if you can find this out, other places that have adopted similar laws. The process of putting together this paper is just as important as the end product. It helps you and your allies to clarify your knowledge and understanding of the issue so that you can make a better argument for it. The mere existence of a white paper gives you credibility as a thoughtful group of advocates who aren't just making stuff up.

The fact sheet will be an easy-to-read version of the white paper. You'll take all of the research that's related to your issue and condense it into a double-sided, single page that will guide conversations about your issue.

4. Brand the issue. Ever heard the slogan "Just do it!" or seen some-one with a MAGA[1] hat? Think about branding as a way to name, frame, and package your issue to make it immediately recognizable and memorable.

5. Map out possible supporters and detractors. To plot your strategy, you'll create two maps of your possible allies and oppo-nents. One will be a map of prominent people and organizations in the community who you think will be in favor of or opposed to your idea, along with the arguments you believe they'll make for or against you. (Yes, supporters and detractors will be on the same map.) The other map will do the exact same thing with legislators.

These maps will be working tools that can help you and your merry band of advocates identify those people and organizations you should approach to help with your campaign. It will also help you think through the arguments your opponents are likely to make and how you can frame a response to their concerns. I know this step may sound a little overwhelming right now, but trust me, I'll show you how to do it in a way that's both easy and makes sense for your campaign.

6. Form a coalition. If I were a betting woman, I'd guess that there hasn't been a law in the history of time that got passed because a handful of people made noise all by themselves. Coalitions are super important to passing laws because you need to show legislators that a whole bunch of folks support your idea. In addition, when you put together a coalition, you'll want to recruit the broadest possible types of people and organizations. That way, you can demonstrate

---

1. For those of you who slept through the Trump campaign and presidency, MAGA is the acronym for Make America Great Again.

to those folks you're lobbying that your group represents more than just the "usual suspects."

7. Develop educational materials. These materials will be the "dummies' guide" to your cause. They'll include simple talking points and strategies that people working on your issue can use to take action on your behalf—such as making a phone call to a city councilor or state legislator—without having to do a lot of extra work.

8. Launch a media campaign. In this day and age, your campaign will need to attract mainstream media and be visible on social media as well. You'll use your research and brand to tell the world why this issue is important and what action is needed to make it right.

9. Approach elected officials. This is when you'll actually lobby! It may sound a little scary, but most people find it to be productive, gratifying, and even fun.

10. Monitor progress on the issue. Once you find a legislator to take up your cause, you will have to be "on it" to help that person move the ball down the field until you reach your goal. I'll outline a path and a strategy for you in Chapter 12.

One thing you may have noticed while going through the steps is that the list is, well, not really a list. What that means is that you can't go through and check off each item when it's "done" (sorry). As you move forward with your campaign, you'll revisit some of these steps as you refine your ideas and involve more people. As confusing as this may sound now, it should make more sense to you as each chapter unfolds, and even greater sense still when you actually use this model to create your own campaign. If you think of it like dance steps, that might help (do I hear the Village People singing and jiggling to YMCA?).

Chapter 3

Step 1: Identify an Issue

Right now, you may be thinking, "Jeez, I'm going to just skip over this chapter because it's a no-brainer." It's certainly easy when the issue you want to work on is literally staring you in the face because folks in your neighborhood, colleagues at other organizations, people you play softball with, or anybody else who is affected by the thing you want to change keep telling you about a problem they encounter time and again. The problem is so obvious, and screams out for a solution that is also so obvious, you end up saying to yourself, "Why in the world hasn't anyone done anything about this? There ought to be a law!"

At that point, you may think you've nailed the issue and are ready to move on to Step 2 (Research the Issue). However, if you do, you might make a rookie mistake by stumbling out of the gate into the warm embrace of *groupthink*.

Groupthink is when your neighbors, friends, and work colleagues are so like-minded you can't imagine that there will be people who don't view the issue the exact same way you do (that's a major reason why this country is so politically divided). To avoid falling into that trap, you need to do a reality check with people outside your circle of allies to make sure that folks who aren't your same age and don't look like you view the problem the same way. The key to this is, ironically, *not* to be an advocate but to listen actively to what others are saying. Your job here isn't to convince these people that an issue is real; it's to figure out whether or not *they* feel the issue is real (and could be addressed by the solution you're proposing). The main objective is to make sure that you're not operating in an echo chamber.

Let's use an imaginary example: A group of neighbors want the city to fence off part of a nearby park so that their dogs can roam free and sniff each other's butts. If all of those dog lovers live close to the park, chances are they would agree it was a great idea; however, families with kids might not like the idea of losing some of their play space, the park's next-door neighbors might worry about barking dogs and smelly poop, or elderly folks might hate the idea of losing a peaceful place to read a book. The dog lovers would need to talk to those other kinds of neighbors to test out their idea. That kind of fact-finding would enable the group to see if there was enough support for their proposal and, if not, what kind of compromise, if any, would be acceptable to others in their community.

While it's not as easy to find common ground when you have differing opinions, a diverse group is generally more representative of society as a whole. Therefore, the ideas you generate because of that diversity are often quite good. They appeal to a broad spectrum of people. This is a lost art in this day and age when many of us get news through a social media chorus that only sings the tunes we like; however, if done well, it pays dividends.

At the same time, there's no need for you to arrive at consensus. If, for instance, most representatives of a diverse group, like a neighborhood association of dog-and-park lovers, agree to a particular solution but a few members keep arguing another viewpoint (driving everyone else crazy), it's perfectly OK to decide to move in the direction of the majority. That assumes that the majority is also a diverse group. In other words, if 9 out of 12 members agree with one another because they *all* own friendly dogs and live near the proposed dog park or, conversely, no one owns dogs, all have kids, and a few live next door to the park, you haven't achieved your goal. The idea is not for everyone to hold hands and sing "Kumbaya"; it's to get sensible ideas passed into laws that appeal to most citizens.

There will also be magical times when you'll be surprised by how much everyone you talk to agrees with you. The issue and its solution are obvious to you and everyone around you; it's just that no one else thought to do something about it before you came along (or thought they *could* do something). It might be relatively easy to fix, but no one in your circle understands how the lawmaking process works (quick, get them a copy of this book!). Sometimes things need to be fixed because a law was passed that didn't anticipate the negative way it would impact a bunch of people, and all of a sudden folks are finding themselves caught up in a situation that needs to be tackled by amending that law, or repealing it altogether. The bottom line is this: If you think something needs fixing and many others think so too, it probably does.

There is one glaring exception to the "obvious problem/simple solution" issue, which is when the solution you're thinking of involves money.

Which it probably will.

SHOW ME THE MONEY

Money and public policy go hand-in-hand in ways that aren't always obvious.

For example, what if you, along with other folks in your apartment building, use the 10 Steps to put together a successful campaign that results in a city ordinance prohibiting smoking in residential buildings with more than 10 units. After you fist bump each other and toast with a celebratory beverage, the fun begins for the city! Someone will be tasked with making sure that new regulations are issued and followed, and that someone will be a city employee (or two, or three, or four . . .) who figures out the best administrative process for notifying apartment building owners about the law, determining what kinds of signs need to be posted, responding to calls from concerned tenants and landlords, determining procedures and timelines for inspections, and establishing a policy for how fines get levied when necessary. All of those things cost money.

When you are lobbying the government to implement a new policy or program, your efforts will be more effective if you have an idea of how it might pay for whatever it is you want done. At the very least, you'll want to show you understand that what you're proposing will require resources such as staff time.

Citizen lobbyists often come with an attitude: "I'm a tax-payer and I pay your salary." But the truth is you're only paying for a fraction of what the government provides, and if you're being honest with yourself, you know that's true. In fact, the only consistent thing about government budgets is that they are unreliable. Sometimes they are tighter than the swimsuits on Olympic athletes; during times when the economy is good, they have more wiggle room. If you go into a meeting with your city councilmember talking about funding your idea by reallocating money from waste, fraud, and abuse, that person is likely to nod politely while doing everything in their power not to roll their eyes (regardless of what political party they represent and what platform they ran on). The truth is, it's hard to find fat even when it's just a teeny bit of money, since other people are also asking for things that cost money, and it adds up quickly. Don't use that as a default strategy. It won't work.

While you aren't expected to become a budget expert, your idea will be better received if you have a broad understanding of how the budget of the government entity you're lobbying operates. The great thing about this type of budget information is that it's pretty easy to access on the Internet. In addition, many helpful people who work in support positions for key policymakers would be happy to explain it to you. It's good if you can do this digging, because the more you know about the constraints your policymakers face, the more open they'll be to your ideas. If you don't show any understanding of what they're dealing with and the difficult choices they have to make, they're probably not going to take your idea seriously. You might as well say, "I'd like you to make it rain marshmallows."

Having a basic understanding of how the budget works might help you come up with a proposal for how that agency could pay for the cost of implementing your idea. In some cases, you might be able to argue that government will actually *save* money if your idea is implemented. That's of course ideal. Then there is that magical word *fee*, which sounds a lot like the dreaded word *tax* and therefore turns off a lot of people. In the apartment building case, you'd of course want to find out about any existing fees landlords already pay to the city. Perhaps those fees could be increased a tiny bit? Maybe you and your fellow campaigners would even consider asking the city to impose a small public safety fee that could be tacked on to a tenant's monthly rent payment for this purpose?

You can also try offering your idea in the form of a pilot program so that the economic consequences of it will be short-lived if the measure doesn't prove to be successful. In rare instances, you might have to say, "This thing is so critical to the health and well-being of people that extraordinary means need to be found to pay for it." In difficult economic times, that is obviously the hardest argument to make and has the least chance of succeeding.

THE EXCEPTION TO THE RULE

There is always an exception to every rule. New ideas that carry high price tags sometimes become law at lightning speed when there is a groundswell of community support. In situations when there is a public outcry for government officials to *do something and do something now*, legislators can jump to make changes that, to be honest, don't always make sense.

To give you an example, California legislators passed a bill that was dubbed *Chelsea's law* in memory of a teenager who had been raped and murdered by a paroled sex offender. It was a horrible and sad crime that became even sadder when the perpetrator confessed to murdering another teenage girl the year before. As you can imagine, hundreds of people—classmates, friends, neighbors, folks in surrounding communities who were angry and heartbroken by what had occurred—turned out for candlelight vigils and marches. Everyone asked how such a thing could have happened. Almost immediately, a core group began to think about legislative solutions for making sure that nothing like that would *ever* happen again.

The state legislator who represented the district where Chelsea lived was fired up with rage about the crime. He immediately proposed legislation that would lengthen the prison terms of sex offenders (some would now get "life"), put many of these criminals on lifetime parole with GPS tracking, extend parole periods for other offenders to 20 years (with an option of indefinite extension), mandate new polygraph technology to test their likelihood of reoffending, and require new types of treatment.[i] You might have read that and thought, "That makes perfect sense to me; let's lock up those monsters and throw away the key!" But before you let those words out of your mouth, let's take a step back for a minute.

It's important to note that this legislation was passed during a horrendous economic downturn, when California was forced to cut $20 billion from its budget. The state's prison agency and California's impartial Legislative Analyst's Office estimated the bill would cost hundreds of millions of dollars in the succeeding years. Think about the extra prison costs, extra costs for treatment, extra parole officers, and so on, and ask yourself if those expenditures are more important than, say, funding domestic violence shelters and in-home services for low-income disabled adults, both of which the Governor's budget had practically wiped out that same year.

In addition, the facts weren't on the side of Chelsea's law. Study after study, including research conducted by the US Bureau of Justice Statistics, showed that only 3.3% to 5% of sex offenders were repeat offenders—figures that are far lower than those for other types of repeat crimes.[ii] Chelsea's law sailed through the legislature despite these facts because it rode on a wave of public outrage about the crime.

The lesson here is that some laws get passed because of widespread public sentiment. Sometimes that's a good thing. For example, the Black Lives Matter movement made quick progress in 2020 on many local police-reform measures, such as those outlawing the use of chokeholds and no-knock warrants and those requiring officers to intervene when a colleague uses excessive force—all because of popular citizen protests. My guess is that many more progressive laws will result from this groundswell of citizen activism. If you can harness that type of energy to promote your cause, then you've got a good chance of creating a new law.

In most cases, though, it's not that easy to pass new laws because legislators tend to spend lots of time weighing the pros and cons of ideas that are brought before them. As part of that process, they carefully consider whether the cost of implementing a law is worth the benefit to be gained. We'll explore that idea in greater detail as the 10 Steps unfold.

IT'S NOT ALWAYS SO EASY

Sometimes you'll identify an issue that a bunch of people recognize as being a problem, but none of you can put your fingers on a way to fix it for all the money in the world. When that's the case, you or someone in your group should spend time researching other legislation or policy that deals with a similar issue as that might spark your thinking about potential solutions. So, how do you do that? Let's say you were working on the campaign to prohibit smoking in apartment buildings. You could start by doing a Google search on cities that have passed similar laws to see what happened in those places. You could also read through independent research reports on the topic written by experts on the subject—in this case, maybe you'd look through research done by the American Cancer Society or the American Lung Association. Later on, you could use what you learned from all of that research to engage in an open-ended brainstorming session with a few friendly public officials about possible ways to approach the problem; however, we're getting ahead of ourselves.

Regardless of whether your problem is obvious or complicated, you'll need to do some type of research on it (something we'll explore in detail in Chapter 4). The reason you need to do digging and detective work is that your first-hand experience or opinion by itself, no matter how brilliant or articulate you are, will not be enough to convince policymakers that your idea needs to become law.

OK, so let's say you have an "in your face" problem; where do you begin? To show you how, we are going to tell you about an actual legislative campaign that was carried out by a group of concerned citizens. None of them had any previous experience lobbying or working with public officials on any type of policy issue. It is safe to say that before I met them (and coached them through this process) they had complete amnesia about basic civics.

Annamarie Maricle and Travis Degheri will take the narrative from here to describe a real-life citizen-advocacy campaign they and a few friends led using the 10 Steps. Here, and in the other nine steps that follow, they'll use their own words in the *How They Did It* sections to describe what happened.

HOW THEY DID IT

Annamarie Maricle:

Our story starts with a course that Pat taught. It was designed to teach people who worked for nonprofit organizations how to lobby. We were her students. Our assignment for the course was to create a full-scale advocacy campaign. Even though we were lucky enough to be taught by the master, we want to assure you that if you follow the 10 Steps, you can really and truly pass a law just like we did.

Our first assignment was for each of us to bring a few ideas for advocacy campaigns to the class that we could share with each other. It was the very beginning of our process to *identify the issue*. The goal was for us to form small teams of people (none of us had any previous experience—we knew nothing about advocacy and lobbying) who would work together to do each step of the process outlined in this book.

I was surprised (and terrified) when one of my ideas struck a deep chord with other people in the class. At the time, I was a single parent grappling with how to help my son, Jack, a bright but troubled teen struggling with substance abuse. I knew that he and several of his friends, all suffering from addiction, had started out by experimenting with DXM (dextromethorphan), a mind-altering drug that was readily available in local grocery stores and pharmacies. It is commonly referred to as "the poor man's PCP" because of its hallucinogenic-like high.

DXM is the active ingredient in many commonly used cough and cold medications. When used as intended, it is a safe and effective treatment. Unfortunately, I didn't realize that my son was one of the more than 400,000 California teens who were using DXM to get high.

When I started researching DXM so I could talk about the issue with others, I discovered a boatload of information about how this seemingly harmless remedy—one that many of us kept in the house for cold and flu symptoms—was being used by children (and adults) who wanted a quick, inexpensive high. It was an easily accessible hallucinogenic drug. I discovered websites that offered detailed instructions for getting high on DXM, with first-hand accounts that might appeal to young teens. I learned that kids often referred to DXM as "Skittles"—after the popular candy that Jack had enjoyed since grade school. Many young people, like Jack, thought DXM was safe because it was legal and easy for them to get. My research also uncovered chilling accounts from parents whose children had died after overdosing on DXM.

When it was time to present my research in class, I felt very anxious. One of my primary coping mechanisms for juggling

continued from previous page

work, school, and parenting was to always keep each area of my life carefully compartmentalized. I was reluctant to share too much about the personal problems that had derailed my son's life with people I had just met. However, when I described this issue to others in the class—it resonated. It resonated because addiction is such a widespread societal problem. It destroys families regardless of race, religion, political affiliation, status, or income. The idea of working on this issue was quickly selected for an advocacy campaign.

Although DXM was not designated as a "gateway" drug, it was clearly dangerous when abused. In my son's case, DXM was the first step on a harrowing path that began in middle school and later included many "harder" drugs. Legislation to stop the sale of DXM to minors would not be enough to stop the devastating trauma caused by drug abuse, but it was an important step that could save lives. Like most people in today's world, Travis and the other members of our team also had friends or family members who had suffered from addiction. When I forced myself to share this extremely scary and difficult challenge that I was trying to manage on my own, they immediately wanted to step in and help.

Travis Degheri:

When I was asked why I wanted to work on this project, I told everyone that Annamarie's passion inspired me. Passion evokes passion. Annamarie's experience with the issue at hand made it real; it made it relevant for all of us. Though many of us didn't know anything about the impact of DXM and how it was being abused by minors, after hearing her talk about it, it all seemed so simple: We needed to change the law to prohibit minors from being able to purchase DXM. Our path to identifying the issue was very straightforward; we were able to recognize how widespread the problem was and to quickly figure out a way that the legislature could address it.

REFERENCES

i. Hall, M. T. (2010, June 29). Chelsea's law adds treatment, assessment. *The San Diego Union-Tribune*. Retrieved September 9, 2021, from https://www.sandiegouniontribune.com/sdut-chelseas-law-adds-treatment-assessment-2010jun29-htmlstory.html

ii. Langan, P. A., Schmitt, E. L., & Durose, M. R. (2003, November). *Recidivism of sex offenders released from prison in 1994*. Retrieved March 16, 2011, from http://bjs.ojp.usdoj.gov/index.cfm?ty=pbdetail&iid=1136

Chapter 4

Step 2: Research the Issue

In lobbying and in life, we'd be nowhere without friends. Creating a lobbying campaign isn't something you can do by yourself—it takes a group of people who are committed to making change. That's even more important if you're dealing with an issue that's very personally and emotionally charged like the DXM campaign. Which leads me to quote singer Peggy Lee, who belted out, "If that's all there is, my friends, then let's keep dancing."

Have you ever done *any* kind of dancing—swing, country, hip-hop, line dancing, ballroom, salsa, the hora, whatever? If you have, you're a great candidate to learn the 10 Steps of effective lobbying because it's just like dancing: The tasks in one step lead to the next and sometimes double back. And like dancing, if you study your moves carefully, you'll step on fewer toes and look better look in the end.

In the first step, you spoke to people outside of your immediate circle to get a sense of whether they agreed that the problem/opportunity you identified was real and should be addressed. You or someone in your group might have also poked around to do some preliminary fact-finding. Now that you've determined your issue is something that others are concerned about it, it's time to move on to more intensive research.

HOW IT'S DONE

Step 2 is focused on learning as much as possible about the issue you want to advance and documenting what you've learned. You don't have to have a college degree to be a good researcher. The most important things to have are good detective skills and good organizational skills. During this step, you'll assemble the cold hard facts of your case, identify potential legislative solutions,[1] and use that information to persuade potential allies, members of the general public, and lawmakers that action needs to be taken. This type of research can take many different forms.

As you read through this chapter, think about how you might divide up various research tasks among a group of friends, colleagues, neighbors, or like-minded citizen activists. Ideally, you've come across these folks during the first stage of identifying the problem or issue to be addressed. Sometimes you can stumble upon existing advocacy groups or other organizations that are wrestling with the same issue and have already done terrific research on it. As a bonus, these folks might eventually agree to become part of your coalition, or your group could become part of theirs. In other words, even though coalition building isn't on our radar until we get to Step 6 in Chapter 8, you need to be thinking about the dance steps that are a few moves ahead.

For reasons that are hopefully obvious to you, you can't wage any legislative or policy campaign simply by talking about a feeling you have that something isn't right and needs to change. This is true even if you've directly experienced whatever the issue is. You have to demonstrate to the people whose support you want that the

---

1. These could be common-sense ideas that come from your own brain or ideas that you discover from doing research on laws that have been passed in other places on the same topic.

problem is big, that it's affected a lot of people, and that there's a way the government can help. It's ideal if you can refer to independent reports, studies, and statistics that illustrate the magnitude of the problem in a way that is easy for the average person to grasp. In the process of doing this research, you'll learn a lot more about the issue yourself, which will make it easier for you to talk about with legislators when the time comes.

Librarians are good friends to make when you do research because they are trained to know a little about a lot of different subjects—especially data sources. Not only can they recommend different sources of information to you—like census data, crime reports, etc.—they can also show you the easiest way to use these files to get the information you need.

Universities are great places to find research on a huge variety of topics, and more often than not, the professors who are engaged in that research are truly happy to share what they know with you. As a recovering academic, I can tell you that most faculty members jump for joy when actual members of the public are interested in their work. The best ones can explain it in a way that makes sense to real people. To find them, go to the website of your local college or university and search for a department that seems like a good match for your topic—for example, environmental studies, health and human services, urban planning, public administration, engineering, etc. Once you find the right department, go to the faculty directory and look up the research interests of the professors. If one of them has written a paper or two on your topic, send them an email or call them to talk about your campaign idea (and don't worry if you can't understand everything they've written—you'll be fine as long as you're clear on their main points).

When you start digging for information on your topic, you'll likely find yourself buried in an avalanche of material. The tricky part is sorting through the documents that support your case and boiling them down to one document that is easy to digest (that part comes later). Start by gathering all the information you can find on the topic and then winnow it down as your campaign takes shape.

HAS ANYONE DONE THIS ANYWHERE ELSE?

The next phase of your research involves doing a simple Google search to find out if there have been any previous attempts, both successful and unsuccessful, to pass a law like the one you're thinking of proposing—either in your state or in the county, city, or town where you want the law made or changed. That search will probably lead you to articles, news stories, and websites of organizations that have worked on the issue or a related one.

If you do find a match—or something that is darn close—you'll want to dig deeper to put your hands on the actual legislation (the copy of the bill) that was filed. Most state governments have online search engines that can help you do this research easily—it will vary more widely at the county or city level. If you have trouble figuring out how to do that search, your local librarian or volunteers at organizations like the League of Women Voters will teach you how to navigate the system. Who sponsored the bill? How long ago? What did it look like? Is the language pretty close to what you've been thinking about or off the mark? You'll eventually want to learn what happened by talking to people who were involved in the effort.

If the bill failed to pass, you'll want to know who opposed the idea and what were their reasons? Did it fail because most members of the city council belonged to one political party, but now a majority of the members belong to a different party? If so, your chances for a re-do may be good.

You can sometimes find detailed records of what happened. At the state level, the policy analyst of the committee to which the bill was assigned will provide you with a treasure trove of information. For example, if it is a bill about health, the Health Care Committee Analyst may be able to provide you with a complete summary, including letters of opposition and support in the bill file. Studying the opposition arguments will provide you with invaluable clues about how to shape your own ideas and lobbying campaign so that you don't make the same mistakes.

You'll also be surprised at how often similar efforts have been attempted in *other* parts of the country (it's been said that "great minds think alike") and at the innovative ways folks have addressed the very same issue through policy or legislative means. If something similar passed in another state, you should get ahold of the legislation that passed there. If the language is dense and somewhat confusing to you, search for news articles that describe the bill and look at the websites of organizations that fought for the legislation; those will help you decipher what was in the bill. You may find a handful of states have passed similar legislation, and if so, you'll probably see slight variations on a theme. These will help you think through what's possible in your area. The Internet makes this kind of work easy to do.

The added bonus is that your research will often lead you to key people in other states or localities who were successful in getting that legislation or policy passed. Many of them will be passionate advocates for the cause who will talk your ear off because they'll be so eager to help you do something similar in your area. The advocates can also let you know how the implementation of the legislation is working, which may or may not lead to information about things that they would have included or done differently had they known about them originally.

WHAT'S IT GOING TO COST?

We've already talked about how there's an excellent chance that whatever it is you're proposing to do will cost the government money. Legislation that has been enacted and implemented in other states (just substitute the word *county, city,* or *town* if that's your focus) will provide you with a gold mine of data on costs. You'll be able to use that information to estimate the cost of carrying out your idea.

For instance, if Colorado has 200,000 people that are affected by *that* problem and your state has 400,000 people that are affected by *that* problem, then you might calculate it would cost your state twice as much to address *that* problem. You need to dig a bit deeper, though, to understand exactly how Colorado is addressing the problem. Maybe Colorado has a sophisticated computer database or some other mechanism like a network of offices in every county of the state that are open on late evenings and Saturdays to provide eligibility screening for *that* service—or whatever it is that makes it relatively easy for Colorado to provide *that.* If your state is not set up this way, you'll need to determine if additional and, therefore, more costly measures would have to be put into place to make a similar idea work in your area.

The bottom line is that you need to figure out as best you can what it would cost your state, county, or city to provide *that.* This is commonly referred to as a *cost-benefit analysis.* You need to be honest with your calculations because, if you're not, the legislators you're lobbying will see through your flimsy math in no time flat and turn their backs on your campaign. You may have the most fabulous idea in the world, but if it costs too much money, chances are that no one will buy it. If you dig as deeply as you can and ultimately can't determine how to calculate what it would cost, be honest about that as well.

COLLECTING YOUR OWN DATA

Sometimes you must go out and collect the data you need—in other words, do your own research—in order to do a cost-benefit analysis of your idea, because no one has done it before. You might be thinking, "Whoa, I have no clue how to do that," but honestly, it doesn't take a rocket scientist to collect data and you can keep the math simple. Collecting data might, for example, involve a simple survey of people in your neighborhood. The trick here is to make sure that you think carefully about the questions that need to be asked of folks so that you don't have to go back and do it a second time. The questions will also need to be asked in such a way that the results won't be challenged later on. It doesn't have to be overly complicated, but it does have to be unbiased and accurate.

For example, if you ask a question like "Should concerned city residents participate in a residential composting program?" you're going to get a muddied response. Why? Because by adding the word *concerned*, you've implied that people aren't being responsible citizens if they don't answer yes. If you ask the question another way—such as "Do you think city residents should be offered the opportunity to participate in a residential composting program?"— you'll probably get more honest answers.

If you didn't go to college, or you went to college but never took a survey methods course, or you went to college and took a survey methods course so long ago there's mold growing on your textbook (assuming you didn't rent it originally or sell it for $2.50 at the end of the semester), then the best thing to do is ask someone who has good survey skills for help. Again, if you're working on a project outside the hallowed halls of academia, you'll find that it's not hard to locate a friendly professor who will volunteer to help write the survey, and there might even be a class of students who will get involved. If you and members of your group divide up the work, you can get the survey itself done in no time.

The time you spend documenting the extent of the problem will benefit you later on. If you are a neighborhood volunteer (bless you!) and you survey a bunch of other neighbors who agree that something must be done, that will have a big impact on the lawmakers you eventually lobby. In the process, you'll probably also identify other folks who are eager to help out.

An awesome example of the importance of data gathering took place in an advocacy campaign that was conducted by the New York Public Interest Research Group. Their campaign was centered on the importance of having the city invest in planting and maintaining street trees. To make their case, the advocates organized a group of volunteers to carry out a unique survey of neighborhood trees. According to an article on the effort that appeared in *The New York Times*:

> Unlike many tree tallies, this one compiled extensive information with an ambitious goal some tree-huggers might consider crudely capitalistic: to break down each tree, its parts and its labor, into dollars and cents. Money has yet to grow on trees, but trees can provide crucial de-pollution services quantifiable in cold, hard cash.
>
> Most broadly, the survey concluded that the 322 trees had an average value of $3,225 per tree and a total value of $1,038,458. The value was said to be the amount the city would have to pay to replace the tree. The most expensive one, a 214-year-old tulip tree on Fillmore Street on Staten Island, came in at $23,069, while a scrawny 6-year-old ginkgo on Hunts Point Avenue in the South Bronx brought up the rear, at $54.

The advocates were so successful with their campaign that the Parks Department's chief of forestry and horticulture thought to use the survey model citywide. She said, "People always knew there was some vague benefit to trees, but you could never quantify it. But once you have the methodology to equate trees with dollars, now you're talking. It's no longer about hugging trees because they're good, but because you have hard data in a language more effective in the public dialogue."[i]

The campaign worked because the advocates thought carefully about the best cost-benefit strategy for making their case. They didn't want to appeal only to people's love of trees; they also wanted to make a good economic argument in their favor—trees lower pollution, which results in less asthma, fewer hospitalizations, etc.—and, with a little ingenuity, ended up doing just that. In addition, by framing the campaign that way, they were able to bring together tree huggers, health advocates, and fiscal conservatives.

All that said, don't get too hung up if you can't figure out a way to put an exact dollar amount on your idea. What you need to know fundamentally is how the idea would work structurally in order for policymakers and their aides to help you understand whether the concept would be doable. For instance, state workers might be able to let the public know about *that* during the same hours when they process applications for some other service.

MAKING IT REAL: PUTTING FACE ON IT

As you go through this process—talking with and listening to people, sorting through what's been done in other places, and documenting the problem—you will invariably find some people (perhaps yourself) who have been directly affected by the issue. It is important to gather their stories because that is what puts a "human face" on your issue and makes it compelling. For instance, when we hear a news story about a natural disaster, the reporters usually start out by talking about the magnitude of the hurricane or the extent of the flooding, but what draws us into the tragedy are the stories of people who have been affected by that disaster. We look at them and think "That could have been me" or "That woman on the raft looks just like Aunt Betty—hey, wait a minute; it *is* Aunt Betty!" The facts of any case always need to be balanced by the impact of the problem or, in some cases, more optimistically, the magnitude of the benefits that people would gain if something were to change. Be sure at the very least to get quotes from people, even if they don't feel comfortable allowing you to use their full name or picture.

I can't state this plainly enough: You'll want people who have experienced the issue first hand, or who will be directly affected by whatever law you want to pass, to be key players in your campaign.

LOBBYING YOUR OWN ORGANIZATION

Those of you who work for a nonprofit know there are often situations when staff people disagree about whether a problem is such a big deal that it needs to be addressed through policy or legislative change. Nonprofits resist the idea of working on broad policy changes for a variety of reasons. These include being ignorant of the legal rights nonprofits have to lobby,[2] thinking that lobbying might be a misuse of the agency's funds, or believing that lobbying isn't

2. For those readers who work or volunteer at a nonprofit and want to know more about the legal lobbying rights of nonprofits, see the Appendix on that topic.

within the mission of the organization. Sometimes there may be leaders at an agency who don't believe the issue you have identified is affecting enough people that it warrants a push for change. These folks might feel that the time you spend trying to arrive at a legislative or policy solution will take you away from your primary job responsibilities. You'll go around in circles with that discussion until you engage in some basic fact-finding to verify your instincts.

Fact-finding to build your case might involve steps such as surveying caseworkers at your organization and others like it to see how many are encountering *that* problem on a regular basis, or conducting focus groups with community members or clients to see how many are dealing with *that* problem, or going door to door to survey how many neighbors have *that* problem. If you're working at an agency, it would be wonderful if your boss gave you permission to gather this information during work hours. If your boss says no, you'll have to do it on your own time, although maybe you can find a good-hearted, community-minded volunteer who will help.

If you can document that there is, in fact, *that* problem, then your supervisor, upper-level manager, board, or whomever it is you need to convince that it's important for your organization to work on this issue will be more likely to give you the go-ahead. The best way to follow up with those resisters is have people who see or experience this issue on a regular basis act as internal advocates. For example, you could encourage social workers at your agency to bring up the issue at a staff meeting. Alternatively, or in addition, you could have community members or clients raise the issue in other ways. Then, it's not just you saying this is a problem (with the eye roll and deep sigh from the higher-ups that says, "There she goes *again* . . . "); you're having other people voice their concerns. Your data will back up the extent of the problem.

Even if they still don't go along with the idea that your organization should lobby on this issue, the process of reaching out to other organizations to see if their clients are also having *that* problem may uncover someone else who is enthusiastic about taking it on (ideally with agency leaders who agree to do something about the situation). Or someone else might end up being a client or community member who realized through your outreach that they weren't the only one dealing with *that* problem. Ultimately, the information you've gathered will be useful in the advocacy campaign, and those people you identified will be critical to its success. In fact, you won't be able to do a good job shaping your ideas and advancing your campaign without them. Legislators are moved by facts, figures, and stories from real people.

Speaking of real people, let's go back to Annamarie and Travis who will continue on with their story.

HOW THEY DID IT

We knew that we needed to learn a lot more to begin to move the issue forward. For us, this meant two things:

1. Determining if similar legislation prohibiting the sale of DXM to minors had already been proposed or passed in other states.
2. Gathering statistics to support our cause, which would illustrate the need for legislation to tackle the problem.

A quick Internet search told us that other people had already tried to address this same issue several years earlier—both in California and other states. In 2003, legislation was introduced

---

continued from previous page

in Texas and North Dakota to prohibit the sale of DXM to minors, and in 2004, a similar bill was introduced in California. Each one was defeated. These bills had been proposed back when Annamarie's son was still in elementary school. If California's had passed, it would have been *much* more difficult for Jack and his friends to start abusing DXM. Knowing that lit a fire under us to continue our research.

That first attempt to pass a law restricting the sale of DXM in our home state was authored by Joe Simitian, a member of the California State Assembly[3] who had sponsored a "There Oughta Be a Law" contest. The winning idea was proposed by Wayne Benitez and Ron Lawrence, who were both with the Palo Alto Police Department at the time. Although Simitian sponsored their bill, it didn't gain enough support to pass. However, we discovered that former Assemblymember Joe Simitian was now *Senator* Joe Simitian. This was great news for us, as we thought he would be someone we could approach about authoring a new DXM bill. Looking at the history of the bill that failed to pass also gave us some insight about how we might shape our proposal.

The second part of researching the issue was gathering statistics to help illustrate the need for the legislation we wanted to propose:

- How many young people were using DXM to get high?
- Was this a widespread problem, or was it isolated to a few areas of California?

3. As a reminder, being in the assembly meant he served on the house side of the California legislature.

- What effects does the continued use of DXM have on an individual?
- Does using DXM in high doses lead to other, more dangerous ways of getting high?

We learned very early on that Google was our friend. We searched far and wide for anything and everything that talked about the impact DXM has on minors. We found numerous studies that supported our claim that DXM was being abused by minors, and that it was a dangerous thing for minors to be doing.

Each of the sources we found used statistics to illustrate their points. We knew this would be important for our purposes because numbers sometimes speak louder than words. It is easy to say to someone you are trying to recruit, "We need to solve this!!" However, passion by itself is not enough to convince someone to take action. Numbers, on the other hand, are solid. They are something everyone can understand. For our campaign, numbers represented people—and a large number of people were being affected by DXM abuse (both users and their family members). We knew that numbers were something that the state legislators would respond to. We weren't making general, baseless claims about the problem; we had statistics to demonstrate our points, including statistics about people who lived in *their* communities.

We found this phase to be very important for the rest of the project going forward. The research would help inform our next steps, including the following step, creating a fact sheet.

REFERENCE

i. Kilgannon, C. (2003, May 12). Get that oak an accountant; study puts a dollar value on work done by city's trees. *The New York Times*. Retrieved March 16, 2011, from http://www.nytimes.com/2003/05/12/nyregion/get-that-oak-accountant-study-puts-dollar-value-work-done-city-s-trees.html

Step 3: Create a Fact Sheet

At this point in the process, you and your allies are sorting through mountains of information about the issue you want to advance. You've gathered information from surveys and conversations with people engaged with it, gotten your hands on publications that have documented it, and with luck, discovered other places where a similar law was proposed and passed (or tried and failed). My guess is that your brain is so crammed with facts, stories, and sample legislation that you're having movie-length dreams about everything you've learned. The trick now is to present that information in a clear and convincing way so that everyone you want to influence— people and organizations who could potentially work alongside you, community leaders whose endorsement you want, members of the media, and most important, the legislators you'll lobby—understands why your campaign is important and what it hopes to accomplish.

HOW IT'S DONE

Although this step is called "create a fact sheet," in reality it involves creating two important documents—a fact sheet and a longer white paper/position paper/case statement/policy paper (take your pick and call it what you want). You'll exercise more than a few brain cells to think through what you want these documents to say because they'll drive the messaging of your campaign. Let's talk about each one (see figure 5.1 and the Addendum at the end of this chapter).

The fact sheet may be the single most important piece of information you'll need because it is the SparkNotes or CliffsNotes summary of the issue. It is a single, powerful, double-sided piece of paper that you'll give to *every* person you want on your side (this includes everyone from your mother to legislators). No one needs to tell you that it's hard to get people's undivided attention for more than a few minutes! Your fact sheet needs to be to the point, pull on heartstrings, be organized, and grab the reader's attention (more on that in a minute).

If you are thinking "Paper fact sheet? That's so last century," think again. While you will eventually develop web and social media content for your campaign, at the end of the day when you're lobbying you'll need a document to use at meetings with legislators and their staff that tells your story in a way that's easy to follow, is logical, and strikes an emotional chord. Sometimes the fact sheet is referred to as a *leave behind*. The process of choosing what facts and stories to highlight will also give you a jump start on organizing your website content.

Even though they are listed here as two separate steps, you'll develop the brand for your campaign (Step 4) at the same time you create your fact sheet (Step 3). As I'll explain in detail in Chapter 6, the name you give your campaign will be shaped by the facts you choose to frame your case.

Putting together a fact sheet is both an art and a science. The art involves making it easy for someone to pick up and absorb your key points without getting eye strain. You need to have a clear heading, a clean typeface, bullets, and boxes; make strategic use of boldface and underlining; and generally put together something that is neat, tidy, and eye-catching. My friend Howard, who is a former state legislator, always emphasizes the need for margins that are wide enough for a legislator to take notes in during the meeting. If you have a friend who is talented at graphic design, an appealing logo can help draw attention to your cause (and you might be able to twist your friend's arm to design the entire fact sheet for you). In addition, you'll probably want to include a chart or a graph that documents the problem and, if you can pull it off, photos of people or places that are part of the story.

The science involves distilling all that you have learned about your issue into a single, two-sided sheet. That isn't easy because once you've taken the time to learn all you can about the issue, you'll have a lot of information stuffed into all those nooks and crannies in your brain, which sometimes makes it difficult to pull out the most compelling elements of your presentation. Remember, facts make the case, while emotions spark the drive to create change—you need both elements in your fact sheet.

Make sure your fact sheet includes the following:

1. A title for your campaign.
2. A brief statement of the problem.
3. A clear and brief statement about your proposed solution (please be sure to put this on the front page).
4. Facts that document the problem (which are footnoted on the flipside of the sheet so that the reader knows you didn't invent them). Again, a chart or graph might be helpful to include here.
5. A human-interest story or quotes illustrating the problem. If you are able to post pictures of people who have been affected by the problem, that can be compelling.
6. A list of organizations and prominent people who have signed on to support your issue (this part of your fact sheet will need

to be revised and updated as your coalition grows—see Step 6 in Chapter 8).

7. The name and contact information of at least one person associated with your campaign. This is the person who the legislator, legislative aide, policymaker, and/or media person can contact for additional information and follow up. It almost goes without saying: Make sure the e-mail address you list isn't from an old AOL account that you never check anymore, and that the telephone number you list isn't the one you gave away to your grandmother when you upgraded your cell.

8. The website address for your campaign.

In all of my years of working on lobbying campaigns, I've never seen a fact sheet that was "one and done." Ever. Your fact sheet is going to change over time for a variety of reasons—you'll have more organizations sign on to your campaign as it gets a head of steam; you might want to change the facts you highlight to address the same few questions that legislators keep asking; and your proposed solution to the issue might change slightly due to input you get from policymakers.

THE WHITE PAPER

Those members of your group who have a mind for detail and organization can put their heads together to write the white paper that will be a companion to your fact sheet.

Most elected officials and their aides will want to learn as much as they can about your issue before they make any decision on whether to support your bill. This will be particularly true for those who are considering authoring a bill on your behalf. Those legislators will undoubtably read your position paper from cover to cover because they'll refer to it when they shape the legislative language for your bill. They'll also use that information when *they* lobby other legislators to get on board your campaign. (You'll still need the fact sheet to get their attention the first time you meet to talk about the issue.)

Keep in mind, though, that your position paper should not resemble a major dissertation on the topic: It, too, needs to be fairly concise and well-referenced.

Your position paper should include many of the same elements that are on your fact sheet, such as all those that I mentioned earlier. However, you can and should expand on these in greater detail. The research section should be the most robust—that's where you present a summary of the information you discovered in Step 2, such as publications that document your issue or the extent of the problem, survey results, and stories of people who have experienced it. You can also include charts and graphs that may be too large or too numerous to include in your fact sheet, as well as photos documenting the problem if that makes sense for your particular cause.

Since you've already spent time thinking about how government might pay for putting this idea into action, you'll want to include that in your position paper. If you have any recommendations for how the effort should be implemented, you should add those, too. These might, for example, include proposed program standards, types of data that could be collected while the program is operating, suggestions for community input, or suggestions for program monitoring and oversight. The position paper allows your group the room to expand on your vision of the effort.

If you are able to provide it, copies of legislative language used in other places that *passed* bills similar to what you are proposing will be extremely helpful. If you include those, be sure to have conversations with advocates who lobbied for those bills to make sure that the law is working as well as intended. If it isn't, they might tell you, "If we had to do it over again, we would have added XYZ to the legislation," which will be invaluable information to add to your position paper.

THE 10-STEP TANGO

As you can see, this is where the list of 10 items covered at the beginning of Chapter 3 begin to make a U-turn: How can you put together a fact sheet when you haven't even named the issue or begun to pull together the other members of your coalition? The truth is you need to start with a draft and work up to those other items on the list. Your fact sheet will evolve just as your campaign will evolve—you'll make several drafts along the way. just as Annamarie and Travis did as they were devising their campaign.

HOW THEY DID IT

Our fact sheet (included at the end of this chapter) was probably the most important tool we used in our campaign to stop the sale of DXM to minors. When we wrote the fact sheet, we treated it as though no one would take the time to read our full position paper. So, everything that was important to have in the position paper—everything that we wanted people to know (statistics, issues, etc.)—needed to be presented in the fact sheet in a way that was concise and easy to grasp.

---

continued from previous page

Our team divided up the tasks in a way that would draw on each of our strengths to create the best fact sheet possible. These included creating a compelling campaign title, stating the problem and solution as we saw it, providing background information on the issue, citing relevant studies on the problem, generating social media/branding, and making the sheet itself visually appealing through graphic design work. We knew the title would be a particularly important component because, if we had a memorable title, then, well, it would be remembered. In our case, we used the campaign title—"DXM: 18 and Over-the-Counter"—to match the logo that we designed to tie everything together visually. We'll talk about that a little more in Chapter 6.

Pat encouraged us to remember that the fact sheet is a "living" document we would want to update and change throughout our campaign. This knowledge made it easier for us to get started as we knew that the first version didn't need to be perfect—we just had to get something down on paper!

Our very first draft was a long, disjointed, and incomplete mess. It wasn't well-organized and just kind of rambled along as we tried to fit in everything we were learning about DXM abuse. The list of supporters we had was more of a wish list because we were still figuring out how to build a coalition.

One of the early mistakes we made was going into far too much detail trying to prove that DXM was dangerous by sharing facts and statistics. However, we came to realize that bombarding people with facts wasn't going to strike a chord with those folks we most needed to reach: community members of all ages and other potential advocates who would work with us to persuade legislators to make our idea a law. Facts are important, but knowing how many kids were using DXM didn't give our readers any real, compelling examples about *how* DXM abuse had destroyed the lives of young, vulnerable teenagers. We wanted to inspire others to join us and become active supporters of the cause. Then we found a letter written by the grieving mother and grandmother of a 17-year-old boy who had overdosed on DXM. They had shared his story in a blog to help other families avoid similar tragedies. We thought a quote from this letter would heighten the impact of the facts and statistics, urging readers to take action.

The final version that we shared with potential supporters isn't perfect, but it got people interested in our cause. We were thrilled to see that a lot of the information provided in our fact sheet made it into the official version from the state senator who authored the bill.

(a)

DXM: 18 and Over-the-Counter
Stop sales of DXM to minors
Overdose can cause seizures, coma, brain damage, death...

DXM: 18 and Over-the-Counter is an advocacy campaign **to stop the sales of cough and cold medicines containing Dextromethorphan (DXM) to minors in California. DXM is an active ingredient in more than 140 cough and cold medicines that 5% of American teens use to get high.** [1]

"My son wanted to live, he loved life.
Glenn did not mean to not wake up the next day..."
(From a letter by a grieving parent of a teen who died after overdosing on DXM) [2]

The Problem in California

Products containing DXM are legal over the counter drugs: visible, inexpensive and easily accessible to teenagers.

- *Annually, more than 400,000 Californians, ages 11-17, abuse DXM to get high.* [3]
- *Overdose can cause seizures, coma, brain damage and can kill a first time user!*

The Solution for California

Pass legislation to make DXM less accessible to minors:

- **Stop selling** DXM directly to minors.
- **Require ID** (18 and over government-issued photo identification) to purchase over-the-counter products containing DXM.

California can be a leader in ending DXM abuse. Proposed legislation will <u>save teens' lives with NO COST to the state of California</u>.

Local government and law enforcement will be reimbursed with funds collected through fines:

- Stores violating the age limits will be fined no more than $200 for the first offense, $500 for the second offense and $1,000 per subsequent offense.

Teens who abuse DXM believe it's a "safe high" because it's legal and easily available in the same stores that sell gum and soda. Street names such as Skittles, Robo, Tussin, Velvet, Triple-C, Vitamin D, Red-Devils imply light-hearted, candy-like fun. They don't know that the dangers multiply when DXM is abused with alcohol, prescription drugs or narcotics.

According to the Drug Abuse Warning Network (DAWN) the number of hospital emergency room visits related to DXM abuse increased more than 70 percent from 2004 to 2007. According to the FDA, inappropriate use of the ingredient was linked to nearly **8,000** emergency room visits in 2008.

Figure 5.1 Fact Sheet

(b)

DXM: 18 and Over-the-Counter

Background Information

DXM is a synthetically produced substance that is chemically related to codeine, though it is not an opiate. DXM is used in over-the-counter medicines to raise the coughing threshold of the brain and has replaced codeine as the most widely used cough suppressant in the United States. It is available in capsule, liquid, liquid gelatin capsule, lozenge, and tablet forms.

Most DXM abusers ingest the drug orally, although some snort the pure powdered form of the drug. Abusers ingest various amounts of DXM depending on their body weight and the effect or plateau that they are attempting to achieve. Some abusers ingest as much as 250 to 1,500 milligrams in a single dosage, far more than the recommended therapeutic dose of 10 to 20 milligrams every 4 hours or 30 milligrams every 6 to 8 hours. *"At high enough doses, DXM alone can suppress the central nervous system. If that happens the brain can stop telling [the] lungs to breathe."*[5]

Widespread reports of DXM abuse have warranted monitoring by the Drugs Enforcement Administration (DEA) and it has been suggested that DXM be added to the Controlled Substance Act. Consumer Healthcare Products Association (CHPA) recommends keeping products available over-the-counter for adults and making DXM less accessible to minors through legislation to prohibit sale to those under 18.[6]

Please join the DXM: 18 and Over-the-Counter Coalition
Center for Healthier Communities - Rady Children's Hospital San Diego
Sundt Memorial Foundation

- Send letters to local and state representatives asking for their support
- Follow us on Twitter: @DXM18andOver ◆ www.18andoverthecounter.blogspot.com
- Join us on Facebook: http://www.facebook.com/pages/18-and-Over-the-Counter/160938723950766

Additional Information:

For questions or to join our coalition, please email us at 18andOvertheCounter@gmail.com or call one of the DXM: 18 and Over-the-Counter Coalition organizers:

- Travis Degheri - VVVVVV
- Kelly Holmes - VVVVVV
- Annamarie Maricle - XXXXXX
- Frances Meda - VVVVVV

References
(1)National Drug Intelligence Center, http://www.justice.gov/ndic/pubs11/11563/index.htm
(2)Voices of the Victims, http://voiceofthevictims.blogspot.com/2006/01/dxm-and-death-letter-written-by.html
(3)Stopmedicineabuse.org, http://www.kidsdata.org:80/data/topic/table/child-population-age.aspx
(4)Drug Abuse Warning Network, https://dawninfo.samhsa.gov/files/TNDR/2006-32R/TNDR32DXM.htm
(5)California Department of Alcohol and Drug Programs, http://www.adp.cahwnet.gov/youth/over_counter_drugs.shtml
(6)Consumer Healthcare Products Association Briefing Book for the Meeting of the FDA Drug Safety and Risk Management Committee, September 14, 2010, http://www.fda.gov/downloads/AdvisoryCommittees/CommitteesMeetingMaterials/Drugs/DrugSafetyandRiskManagementAdvisoryCommittee/UCM224448.pdf

CHAPTER 5 ADDENDUM

White Paper

DXM: 18 and Over-The-Counter Coalition

Stop Sales of Cough and Cold Medicines containing Dextromethorphan (DXM) to Minors

DXM: 18 and Over-The-Counter Key Contacts:
Travis Degheri - (XXX) XXX-XXXX
Annamarie Maricle - (XXX) XXX-XXXX
Frances Meda - (XXX) XXX-XXXX

Twitter: @DXM18andOver
http://www.facebook.com/
pages/18-and-Over-the-Counter/160938723950766
18andoverthecounter.blogspot.com
18andOvertheCounter@gmail.com

EXECUTIVE SUMMARY

Dextromethorphan (DXM) is a safe and effective cough suppressant, and accounts for 85–90% of all OTC medicines containing a cough suppressant sold in grocery stores, pharmacies, mass merchandisers, and other retail outlets. When taken as recommended, products containing DXM are safe and effective in suppressing cough symptoms. However, approximately 5% of American teens (an estimated 400,000 in California) report they have used OTC cough and cold medicine "to get high" in the past year.[1] Abusers, who ingest 8-20 times the recommended therapeutic dose, risk serious complications that can include seizures, brain damage, liver damage and death in addition to the dangers associated with mental disassociation.[2]

Teens who abuse DXM may believe it's a "safe high" because it's legal and easily available in the same stores that sell gum and soda. Street names like Skittles, Robo, Tussin, Velvet, Triple-C, Vitamin D, or Red-Devils imply light-hearted, candy-like fun. Minors may be unaware that the dangers multiply even further when DXM is abused with alcohol, prescription drugs or narcotics.[3] Consequently, between 2004 and 2007, emergency room visits associated with DXM abuse rose 70% raising concerns about teen drug abuse, public safety and associated healthcare costs.[4]

1. Suite101.com. (October, 2009). Kids Using Cough Syrup to Get High. Nash, L. Access on November, 3, 2010 from: http://www.suite101.com/content/kids-using-cough-syrup-to-get-high-a135801.
2. Consumer Healthcare Products Association Briefing Book for the Meeting of the FDA Drug Safety and Risk Management Committee, September 14, 2010, http://www.fda.gov/downloads/AdvisoryCommittees/CommitteesMeetingMaterials/Drugs/DrugSafety andRiskManagementAdvisoryCommittee/UCM224448.pdf .
3. Suite101.com. (October, 2009)
4. Drug Abuse Warning Network, https://dawninfo.samhsa.gov/default.asp

The DXM: 18 and Over-the-Counter Coalition has identified a COST FREE opportunity for California to be a leader in addressing cough medicine abuse through state legislation to stop sales of nonprescription medicines containing DXM to anyone under 18 years of age. The DXM: 18 and Over-The-Counter Coalition is working with the Consumer Healthcare Products Association (CHPA), an organization which advocates for legislation to establish age restrictions on purchase of medicines containing DXM.[5] In 2008, CHPA encouraged the state of New Jersey ban the sale of over-the-counter medications containing DXM to minors(S. 664). While no state has yet enacted a law to stop the sale of these cough medicines to minors, we know from experience that age restrictions can make a successful impact and give parents another tool to monitor what comes into their homes. For example, the Stop Tobacco Access to Kids (STAKE) Act, led to a significant decrease in minors' access: from 41.2% before implementation of legislation (1994) to 12.7% after implementation (1998).[6] Similarly, the DXM 18 and Over-The-Counter Coalition seeks to curb DXM abuse among minors by decreasing minor accessibility of cough medications through an 18 and over age restriction for the purchase of such medicines.

BACKGROUND

What is an Over-The-Counter (OTC) Medication?

Over-the-counter (OTC) drugs are medicines that can be purchased without a doctor's prescription. OTC cough medicines are

---

5. Consumer Healthcare Products Association Briefing Book for the Meeting of the FDA Drug Safety and Risk Management Committee, September 14, 2010, http://www.fda.gov /downloads/AdvisoryCommittees/CommitteesMeetingMaterials/Drugs/DrugSafetyand RiskManagementAdvisoryCommittee/UCM224448.pdf.

6. Tobaccocontrol.com. http://tobaccocontrol.bmj.com/content/9/suppl_2/ii15.abstract

grouped into 2 types: antitussives (or cough suppressants) and expectorants. Dextromethorphan (some brand names: Triaminic Cold and Cough, Robitussin Cough, Vicks 44 Cough and Cold) is the most commonly used antitussive. The only expectorant available in OTC products is guaifenesin (some brand names: Mucinex, Robitussin Chest Congestion). Dextromethorphan relieves cough symptoms by suppressing the cough reflex.[7] Expectorants work by thinning mucus and clearing the mucus from one's airway. Dextromethorphan and guaifenesin are sometimes combined with each other (one brand name: Robitussin Cough DM). They are also available in combination with other drugs, such as pain relievers, decongestants or antihistamines. These combination products are meant to treat multiple symptoms of the common cold at once.[8]

What is DXM?

Dextromethorphan (DXM) is a synthetically produced substance that is an active ingredient found in more than 140 over the counter cough and cold medicines. Dextromethorphan accounts for 85–90% of cough suppressants sold in the US It has replaced codeine as the most widely used cough suppressant in the US and can be conveniently purchased in various forms such as capsule, liquid, liquid gelatin capsule, lozenge, and tablet. When taken at recommended dosages, the drug is effective in suppressing cough symptoms by raising the coughing threshold of the brain.[9] However, DXM produces psychoactive effects when it is ingested in amounts

7. Canning, B.J. Central Regulation of the Cough Reflex: Therapeutic Implications, Pulmonary Pharmacology Therapeutics, April 2009.

8. FamilyDoctor.org, http://familydoctor.org/online/famdocen/home/otc-center/otc-medicines /858.html

9. Consumer Healthcare Products Association, FAQs About Dextromethorphan, 2010. Retrieved from http://www.chpa-info.org/issues/FAQs_Dex.aspx#13.

well above the maximum recommended therapeutic dose. Abusers describe "plateaus" of abused effects related to the amount taken. At high doses, health consequences including nausea, hypertension, emergency room visits, and, in very rare instances, even death, can result.[10] Additionally, when ingested in large doses, DXM can act as a hallucinogenic with grave side effects.[11]

Exampl es of Common Cough and Cold Medicines Containing Dextromethorphan:[12]

Vicks 44 Cough Relief	NyQuil and DayQuil	Tylenol Cold
Dymetapp DM	Robitussin	Mucinex DM
ElixSure Cough Children's	Miltuss	Pediacare
Benylin Pediatric Formula	Silphen DM	Creomulsion
Dexalone	Delsym	Simply Cough
Children's Pedia Care	Nycoff Pediacare Long-Acting Cough	

10. Consumer Healthcare Products Association Briefing Book for the Meeting of the FDA Drug Safety and Risk Management Committee, September 14, 2010, http://www.fda .gov/downloads/AdvisoryCommittees/CommitteesMeetingMaterials/Drugs /DrugSafetyandRiskManagementAdvisoryCommittee/UCM224448.pdf.
11. Anyaegbunam, Jenneifer Adaeze. "Why the FDA must curb cough syrup abuse." MSNBC. com, The Grio, September 2, 2010. Retrieved from http://www.thegrio.com/health/why -the-fda-must-curb-cough-syrup-abuse.php
12. Livestrong.com. http://www.livestrong.com/article/27119-list-cough-medicines/

THE PROBLEM

Teens may be abusing DXM under the false pretense that it is a "safe high" because it's legal and easily accessible. DXM is also an inexpensive high and it does not show up on breathalyzers which makes it appealing for students, as they won't get caught at school dances and functions.[13] Teens may refer to it with street names like Skittles, Robo, Tussin, Velvet, Triple-C Vitamin D and Red-Devils imply candy-like fun, contributing to the misperception that a DXM high is harmless.[14] In fact, websites like www.dextroverse.org, http://psychonauts.tribe.net, or www.erowid.com are devoted to describing how abusers can achieve a desired high or 'plateau'.

Most DXM abusers ingest the drug orally, although there are occasional references to snorting the unfinished powered form of the active ingredient. Abusers ingest various amounts of DXM depending on their body weight and the effect or plateau that they are attempting to achieve. The U.S. Department of Justice / Drug Enforcement Administration Office of Diversion Control includes Dextromethorphan among "Drugs and Chemicals of Concern" and states that abusers ingest DXM in single dosages of 100 to 1,500 milligrams, far more than the recommended dose of 10–20 milligrams every 4 hours or 30 milligrams every 6-8 hours.[15]

---

13. Michael, Jenny. "Household drugs and chemicals being misused by teenagers." Bismark-Mandan News, January 11, 2008. Retrieved from http://www.bismarcktribune.com/news/local/article_07fe9a9a-bc5d-5eed-9341-ce6ed1c81f13.ht
14. Suite101.com. (October, 2009). Kids Using Cough Syrup to Get High. Nash, L. Accessed on November, 3, 2010 from http://www.suite101.com/content/kids-using-cough-syrup-to-get-high-a135801
15. U.S. Department of Justice Drug Enforcement Administration Office of Diversion Control, Drugs and Chemicals of Concern - Dextromethorphan. August 2010. Retrieved from http://www.deadiversion.usdoj.gov/drugs_concern/dextro_m/dextro_m.htm

Side-effects

DXM abuse can cause seizures, coma, brain damage and can even result in death. DXM alone can suppress the central nervous system; if that happens the brain can stop telling the lungs to breathe.[16] Additionally, DXM abuse can cause blurred vision, mental disassociation, numbness of the limbs, and impaired judgment which can lead to accidents and other ills associated with drug or alcohol abuse. For some teens, DXM may be a gateway drug and lead to a long road of drug abuse and self-destructive behavior.

SHORT-TERM SIDE-EFFECTS (6 Hours)	LONG-TERM SIDE-EFFECTS
Mental dissociation and inability to connect thoughts. Hallucinations.	Parents report that DXM abuse can lead to experimentation with other substance abuse
Unconsciousness	Seizure
Nausea and sweating profusely	Coma
Blurred vision and headache	Brain-damage
Numbness in toes and fingers and inability to move limbs	Death
Restlessness	

As noted, overdosing on DXM alone can be extremely dangerous; however some abusers may not realize that when DXM is abused

16. The Partnership at Drugfree.org, http://www.dxmstories.com/facts4.html

with alcohol, prescription drugs or narcotics the dangers multiply. Many of the cold and cough medications that contain DXM also contain other active ingredients, which can cause additional health complications. Side effects of commonly found active ingredient(s), may include increased blood pressure from pseudoephedrine, potential acute liver damage from acetaminophen, and central nervous system toxicity, cardiovascular toxicity and anticholinergic toxicity from antihistamines.[17] High doses of DXM in combination with alcohol or other drugs is particularly dangerous and deaths have been reported.[18] Serotonin syndrome, a potentially life-threatening drug reaction, can occur when DXM is used with antidepressants, including monoamine oxidase inhibitors and serotonin re-uptake inhibitors.[19]

EMERGENCY ROOM VISITS

According to the FDA, between 2004 and 2007, the number of dextromethorphan abuse related emergency room visits increased over 70 percent. In 2008 there were approximately 8,000 emergency department visits involving dextromethorphan.[20] Moreover, curbing DXM abuse can make for a healthier California youth while cutting down on thousands of dollars in medical costs associated with DXM related ER visits and follow-up care.

---

17. Medline Plus at http://www.nlm.nih.gov/medlineplus/ency/article/002636.htm
18. U.S. Department of Justice Drug Enforcement Administration Office of Diversion Control, Drugs and Chemicals of Concern - Dextromethorphan. August 2010. Retrieved from http://www.deadiversion.usdoj.gov/drugs_concern/dextro_m/dextro_m.htm
19. National Library of Medicine Hazardous Substances Database - Dextromethorphan. Retrieved on January 7, 2011 from http://toxnet.nlm.nih.gov/cgi-bin/sis/search/r?dbs+hsdb:@term+@rn+125-71-3
20. Drug Abuse Warning Network, https://dawninfo.samhsa.gov/default.asp

NATIONAL ATTENTION

Widespread reports of DXM abuse reveal that 10% of minors in the United States have abused DXM at least once.[21] The US Government-funded Monitoring the Future survey estimates approximately 5% of 8th, 10th, or 12th graders has abused OTC cough and cold medicine in the past year "to get high."[22] Consequently, DXM abuse has drawn national attention, including a Food and Drug Administration advisory committee meeting on the issue. The question has been raised as to whether DXM should be added to the Controlled Substances Act. In 2003, legislation to stop the sale of DXM to minors was introduced in both the Texas and North Dakota state legislatures without success and similar legislation also failed in California in 2004.[23] Most recently New Jersey has taken the lead on the East Coast and worked with the Consumer Healthcare Products Association to introduce legislation to ban the sale of DXM to minors. At the federal level, discussions are taking place in regard to DXM abuse and proposed legislation to ban the sale of DXM to minors across the United States.

THE SOLUTION

Create legislation to prohibit the sale, without a prescription, of over the counter medicines containing dextromethorphan to a minor (a person under the age of 18).

21. California Poison Control System San Francisco. *Dextromethorphan Abuse in Adolescence: A Rising Trend.* Anderson, I. Accessed in December, 2010 from: www.csam-asam.org/pdf /misc/**DXM**_CSAM_9_07.ppt
22. Monitoring the Future 2009. Institute for Social Research, University of Michigan
23. National Drug Intelligence Center, Intelligence Bulletin: DXM (Dextromethorphan), October 2004. http://www.justice.gov/ndic/pubs11/11563/index.htm

A. Restrictions on the trade of Dextromethorphan

Require all retailers to require government issued photo identification to prove that the purchaser is 18 or over by:

- Make it unlawful for any commercial entity to knowingly or willfully sell or trade to a person under 18 years of age any product containing dextromethorphan.
- Make it unlawful for any person who is less than eighteen years of age to purchase a product containing any quantity of dextromethorphan.

B. Penalties

A commercial entity which knowingly and willfully violates the provisions of this 18 and over law (outlined above) shall be liable to a civil penalty of:

- Not more than $200 for a first violation,
- Not more than $500 for a second violation
- Not more than $1,000 for a third and each subsequent violation.

Please note that In the case of a retail establishment that is part of a chain with two or more locations in the State, the violation shall be assessed against the particular retail establishment and not the chain. Additionally, a retail clerk who fails to require and obtain proof of age for the purchaser shall NOT be guilty of an infraction or charged with individual fines. Rather, the retail store shall be penalized according to the fines established and will have the freedom and choice to set store policies and procedures for clerks and employees who violate the law.

C. Exclusions from this Law

The provisions of this act shall not apply to any prescription medication containing dextromethorphan that is dispensed by a pharmacist pursuant to a valid prescription.

D. Enforcement and Compliance

An official authorized to enforce the State or local health codes or a law enforcement officer having enforcement authority in that municipality may issue a summons for a violation of the DXM 18 and over law.

A penalty recovered under the provisions of this law shall be paid into the treasury of the municipality in which the violation occurred for the general uses of the municipality.

E. Fiscal Effect

There are NO COSTS involved in the proposed legislation as the cost of enforcement by local officials and law enforcement officers will be offset by fine revenues

Unknown sales tax revue loss will likely be offset in whole by reduced healthcare costs paid for by publicly-funded health care programs.

F. Summary

The DXM: 18 and Over-The-Counter Coalition believes that the proposed legislation would be a step towards making cough/cold medicines less accessible to minors for abuse, and provide parents with a tool to help monitor what their teen brings into the home. Such legislation would also deter minors from abusing cough medicine and raise awareness among kids and their parents about the dangers of cough/cold medicine abuse. The misperception that a DXM high is "legal" and therefore "safe" would be lessened through this age restriction legislation.

PARENT TESTIMONIAL

"Six years ago, in 2004, legislation to prohibit the sale of DXM to minors was first proposed in California.

*In 2008, my 14-year-old son [Jonny] and his friends thought DXM would be a fun, safe and easy way to get high. They could walk over to a local drug store or grocery store and choose from a wide selection of over-the counter products containing dextromethorphan. The first time my son overdosed on cough medicine, I was at home and took him to the emergency room before it was too late. He has been to the emergency room 2 more times since that first incident, once after I found him unconscious after he experimented with Robitussin gell pills mixed with alcohol. After being introduced to the DXM high, [Jonny] began his experimentation with other mind altering substances. Most recently, my son was transported to the emergency room by ambulance after overdosing on methamphetamine. A 16 year old should be trying out for the winter musical and playing school sports instead [Jonny] is struggling with reoccurring visits to rehab for his substance abuse addiction. **It all started with DXM.** Now, I want to see California pass legislation to prohibit the sale of DXM to minors because many teens still don't realize that abusing DXM is very dangerous." -AM*

COALITION

Current Coalition Members:	
Center For Healthier Communities at Rady Children's Hospital – San Diego	Sundt Memorial Foundation
California Chapter of the American Academy of Pediatrics (AAP)*	California District Attorneys Association
California School Nurses Organization	Community Alliances for Drug Free Youth (CADFY)
*Consumer Healthcare Products Association	Drug Free San Diego / Communities Against Substance Abuse
Irvine Community Drug Prevention	North Coastal Prevention Coalition
Phoenix House	San Diego Health and Human Services Agency

*While CHPA does not control or formally endorse this campaign, CHPA is advocating for age restrictions for the sale of DXM and is working directly with DXM 18 and Over-The-Counter to advocate for legislation.

Chapter 6

Step 4: Brand the Issue

To recap where we've been thus far along our journey through the 10 Steps, you've read an overview of the Big 10, learned the ins and outs of how to identify an issue, do research on it, and put together a fact sheet and position paper. But if we're being honest with ourselves, we both know that your fact sheet can't be unveiled to the world until you figure out how to *name and frame* your campaign. This is also referred to as giving it a *brand*.

HOW IT'S DONE

The step of naming your campaign—which can also involve framing your issue—is *super* important because it will impact how well your idea "sells" in the marketplace of ideas.

We know that advocacy and lobbying is all about interest groups, which include nonprofits and other types of citizen groups, waging a campaign to persuade elected officials to create or change a law that's important to that group. There's a better chance, though, that legislators will act on an issue if they hear about it from the general public and not just the interest groups directly affected by the issue. If you stop to think about it for a moment, it makes perfect sense: If you are fighting for legislation to improve the rights of a special class of people, like people with disabilities, low-income college students, or the LGBTQ community, you'd want campaign allies to weigh in who were *not* disabled, low-income college students, or LGBTQ. It's especially important for legislators to hear from citizens who live in their district because that's ultimately who they have the responsibility of representing. Therefore, the name of your campaign needs to be easily communicated to a broad audience who can in turn put pressure on their legislators to act.

Obviously, communicating your message to the public is hugely important if you are working on a ballot campaign, which by definition appeals to the voting public as a whole. But unless you believe that you have zero chance of getting a bill through the legislature, you probably won't launch a ballot campaign as your first attempt to pass a law because ballot campaigns are *extremely* expensive.[1]

Great campaign names are like chocolate-and-vanilla-swirl ice cream cones—they consist of two intertwined elements that come together in a fantastic way. In a few words, these campaign names combine a description of the issue with a message that refutes the central argument of those who oppose the idea (this will become clearer in a minute, when we look at some well-known examples). In addition, if you wrap your campaign in a good name, people hearing it for the first time will immediately understand what it's all about and remember it.

Really good *frames* have a way of positioning your issue so that people who tend to look at things from one perspective are drawn instead to consider your point of view. A really good name for an issue can also serve a dual function of framing it as well. Given all of that, you can see why you'll need to have a few strategic brainstorming sessions with your team to invent a name for your campaign.

---

1. Since ballot campaigns aren't the subject of this book, I recommend you visit and learn from the Ballot Initiative Strategy Center (https://ballot.org) if you want to explore this option in greater detail.

Nothing can explain these points better than the following examples of "names and frames" that might be familiar to you from local and national advocacy campaigns:

- **Death Tax**—which has been used for decades to reframe the term *estate tax* (the federal tax on cash, real estate, stock or other inherited assets) and has been so successful that it almost succeeded in wiping out those taxes permanently. Today,[2] 99.8% of estates pay ZERO taxes; you'd have to inherit more than $5.49 million per person—almost $11 million for a married couple—to be hit with a tax bill!

- **Marriage Equality**—which reframed the term *same-sex marriage* and resulted in legalization across many states before the US Supreme Court *Obergefell v. Hodges* ruling made it a national law in 2015. If you look at the history of marriage equality legislation on the state level, it attracted important support from non-LGBTQ, Latinx, African American organizations and legislators because it was framed as a civil rights issue.

- **Climate Change**—which replaced the term *global warming* to describe shifts in climate temperatures due to dramatic increases in greenhouse gas emissions. As of this writing, 23 US states have adopted some form of climate change legislation.[i]

- **Living Wage**—which reframed the term **minimum wage** to describe baseline wages that companies would be required by law to pay (and would presumably allow workers to afford a decent quality of life). Activists passed the first city-wide living wage law in Baltimore in 1990 and went on to make it

2. The last federal estate tax law was passed in 2017 (see https://www.cbpp.org/research/federal-tax/ten-facts-you-should-know-about-the-federal-estate-tax).

statewide in 2007. By 2020, advocates had successfully passed a variety of living wage laws in 29 states[ii] and in 51 cities and counties.[iii]

In each of these cases, the names of those advocacy campaigns offered a frame for an issue that shifted the debate on that topic by asking people to look at it in a different light. The advocates who named and framed these campaigns could have called them anything. They could have thought up long, wordy names or given them one that wouldn't have had such broad appeal. What if, for example, they had called the Living Wage campaign the Move Workers Out of Poverty Campaign? That wouldn't have quite the same righteous ring to it as *living wage*. It is important for you to think strategically about the name of your campaign and what it will mean to people who are listening to it for the first time.

The name of your campaign is its calling card. Often, legislators or other policymakers will refer to the name of your campaign in shorthand, so it's good to invent something that is concise and memorable. Don't rush it: Take your time to think up a good name for your campaign.

HOW THEY DID IT

The name of your cause and how you choose to brand it will help drive your cause forward. Most important, you want it to be remembered. In our case, we bridged two common phrases—"18 and over" and "over the counter—to describe how they relate to the purchase of DXM. The result? We branded our campaign *DXM: 18 and Over the Counter*.

While we felt it was clever to combine two relevant phrases, the most important aspect about our name is what it conveys. It immediately let's someone know what our stance is: We want DXM to be available to those who are 18 and older as long as it is sold "over the counter" (meaning, a clerk would be required to check the ID of anyone purchasing DXM). While some of our internal discussions involved determining if we could make all products containing DXM 100% prescription based, we ultimately decided that this would have had significant pushback from consumers and make it much more challenging to find an author for our bill. With retailers already selling DXM over the counter, our campaign required only one relatively small change—store clerks would need to take a few seconds to check for identification before the drug could be purchased.

Once we settled on a brand name, we were able to apply it to all of our branding efforts such as our fact sheet, Twitter handle, and blog. While we liked our name and the fact that it was "catchy," we did recognize that it was rather long. The longer the name, the harder it would be to remember, and the less traction it might have as a result. Despite these concerns, we still used *DXM: 18 and Over the Counter,* and we are happy we did.

Branding our issue was a big step forward, and it paved the way for our next steps in mapping and building a coalition. In Chapter 5 you can see how we incorporated our brand name into our cause. Admittedly, our examples left something to be desired in a visual sense, but our brand name still served its purpose.

REFERENCES

i.   Center for Climate and Energy Solution. (2021). *State climate policy maps.* Retrieved September 13, 2021, from https://www.c2es.org/content/state-climate-policy/

ii. National Conference of State Legislatures. (2021, April 20). *State minimum wages.* Retrieved September 13, 2021, from https://www.ncsl.org/research/labor-and-employment/state-minimum-wage-chart.aspx#Table

iii. UC Berkeley Labor Center. (2021, July 12). *Inventory of US city and county minimum wage ordinances.* Retrieved September 13, 2021, from http://laborcenter.berkeley.edu/minimum-wage-living-wage-resources/inventory-of-us-city-and-county-minimum-wage-ordinances/

Chapter 7

Step 5: Map Out Possible Supporters and Detractors

Hopefully, you and your friends caught lightning in a bottle and, in the process, created a brilliant and inspiring name for your campaign. If you did, mapping the universe of people and organizations you think will be in favor of or against your idea is the next step.

On the other hand, if your possible campaign name is still spinning around your brain like clothes in the washer, this mapping step might also help you and your friends with the naming process. That's because, as I mentioned in Chapter 6, the arguments your opponents make can also provide important clues about how you might name and frame your issue. So, if you're feeling stuck on Step 4, work on Step 5 and then go back to Step 4. I wasn't kidding when I said this 10-step lobbying model was a dance!

As I mentioned way back in Chapter 2, Step 5 involves creating two maps. First, you'll dive into the process of mapping out your possible supporters and detractors, and then you'll create a second map where you go through the same process with the legislators you'll be lobbying. The idea of mapping legislators may sound a little intimidating, but it's really *much* easier than you might think. I'll explain how to make both of these maps in this chapter.

HOW IT'S DONE: MAPPING SUPPORTERS AND DETRACTORS

Every issue in the world has people who are in favor of it, those who are against it, and those who wouldn't pay attention to it if an elephant roller skated in front of them with a huge banner slung across its body. Within those first two categories—the people for and against the issue—there are lots of shades of gray. Just like hot water that comes out of the faucet, some of these folks will be lukewarm supporters (or opponents), others will be scalding hot activists, and still others will be somewhere in the middle. You and your team will need to think carefully about the range of people and organizations you believe will weigh in for and against your issue.

I like to begin a brainstorming process like this on a whiteboard or big piece of paper where I can draw a map of the players. It doesn't have to be complicated. You can start with a chart that has three simple headings like "Love Our Issue," "Middle of the Road/Don't Know," and "Strong Opposition," under which you scribble in whatever comes to mind. Alternatively, you can go online and download a free Force Field Analysis tool from MindTools (http://www .mindtools.com/pages/article/newTED_06.htm) that will help you and your team develop a map. Regardless of the format you use, as your campaign moves forward, you'll move players from one column to another as you find out who is a real supporter or who has dug in deep against your campaign. Sometimes the results can be surprising in both directions.

At the first mapping meeting, ask yourselves the following questions:

1. *Who do we think is going to be strongly in favor of the idea and could do some heavy lifting for our campaign?*

This list might include several people outside your immediate group who have also experienced the issue and are willing to speak publicly about it, additional organizations that represent groups of people who are concerned about the issue and/or have faced it, and a team of community leaders who can be counted on to mobilize other folks (such as members of their neighborhood group or nonprofit) to contact legislators about the issue.

2. *Who do we think might be in favor of our campaign and could be convinced to actively support it?*

These are folks who care about the issue but won't want to be as involved as the core group. They'll help by doing things like sending out announcements about the campaign through their social media networks and/or listservs and contacting their legislators when you ask them to.

3. *Who is a big deal who might give our campaign a lift if they lend their name or the name of their organization to our campaign?*

It's not just movie and rap stars who make a difference. A single high-profile coalition member with an active membership base of people is worth a ton if that person is willing to sign on to send out e-blast on your issue to their network.

4. *Who do we think is going to be actively against our campaign and why?*

What arguments will they use to try to torpedo our campaign? Who else is part of their network who they might persuade to work against us?

5. *Who do we think might be against our idea but could back down (or, even better, move to our side) if we're able to talk to them about it in a way that addresses their concerns?*

What response do we have to the arguments being made against us that we can easily refute? What key arguments can we use to soften opposition to our idea?

If you're honest with yourselves and think carefully about the arguments the opposition might have, you may be able to put together research to refute or address their objections. If you can find out who weighed in on this issue in the past and what positions they took, that will also help with your campaign strategy. At the very least, you won't be caught off guard later on when detractors come up with arguments against your idea (and you'll be prepared with your own defense). That's why earlier on it was suggested that your campaign team have people on it who have different views or, even better, different affiliations across the political spectrum. If you have a diverse team as you're working through all of the steps described so far, you'll be well aware of what might lie ahead because your group will have already talked about it openly (and maybe even argued a bit, which is fine, too).

If you can't find anyone in your inner circle to talk to who has an opposing view, there's always a (hopefully distant) family member you can call . . .

SUPPORTERS: THINKING BEYOND THE USUAL SUSPECTS

In many campaigns that are led by nonprofits, the coalition of allies consists entirely of other nonprofits that were founded for the same purpose. That's not good for a variety of reasons. For one, policy-makers sometimes think that you're really lobbying for your own self-interest, along the lines of "They're working on that campaign because they won't have a paycheck if their clients don't get services." In addition, if all your supporters represent one type of organization, the campaign will be easier to minimize with statements like "There go those crazy arts people again!"

For those reasons and others, you need to be strategic when you put together your map because it will directly lead to assembling your campaign coalition (Step 6, which is discussed in Chapter 8). The mapping, and the coalition that will take shape as a result, should ideally involve people and organizations that represent many different sectors, such as the business community, the public sector, unions and other grassroots or nonprofit subsectors (for example, environmental groups or corporations working in collaboration with affordable housing groups). This is important because it doesn't make your effort seem as narrow in focus; instead, it has the active support of so many different types of people and organizations. I call these people the "odd bedfellows."

An example of this is the Black Lives Matter movement. When people took to the streets to protest in the spring of 2020, Black Americans led the way but weren't the only people marching. The demonstrations for equality included allies that were White, Asian, Latinx, and LGBTQ people of all colors. That broad-based coalition led to all kinds of people and corporations speaking up, among them army generals, mayors, and corporate CEOs. The pressure caused many rapid policy changes in community policing, such as laws eliminating choke holds, neck restraints, the use of tear gas, and the ability of police to conduct random stops and searches (among many, many others). It also resulted in the removal and banning of Confederate monuments and flags from many public spaces and the renaming of military bases. You could rightfully say that these changes were long overdue (and you'd be correct). My point is that they came about more quickly because many people across society actively expressed their disgust and horror at these racist behaviors and tributes.

The longer the list of your supporters, the stronger your campaign will be. Remember, too, that the map will evolve over time as you meet with and add key players that dot your landscape.

HOW IT'S DONE: MAPPING LEGISLATORS

Charting out legislators who you think might be your allies and detractors is *much* easier than it seems, and it often is even easier than creating the map of the general community. To start, you'll need to go back to the research you did in Step 2 (see Chapter 4) that identified who in the past sponsored similar types of legislation in your target area (for example, city, county, and state) and who opposed it for what reason. That information will be super important to helping you address the concerns of those legislators and opposition groups before someone raises them this time. This research might also help you unearth organizations you missed in the first map of the larger community.

If there's never been a similar legislative or policy proposal in your area, you'll have to do some simple biographical research on each of the legislators you plan to target. If you're scratching your head about how to figure out who should be on that list, think about the Yellow Brick Road I outlined in Chapter 1 that summarizes the road trip an idea takes on its way to becoming a law. In other words, your bill (once you hopefully get a legislator to agree to author it) will begin its journey at a *committee hearing*. Therefore, your lobbying targets are legislators who are *members* of a committee that is likely to consider your bill. Your goal is to get one of those folks— ideally, the chair of the committee—to carry your bill.

To begin, look at the list of committees that your legislative body operates (they'll be the same for each side if you're working on a state issue)—there is bound to be one that seems like it would be a logical fit for your bill. Don't worry: It shouldn't be hard to land on because the committee names are pretty obvious (public safety, environment, transportation, land use, housing, etc.). That said, if you're on the fence about which committee it might be, or whether your bill might be heard in more than one committee, choose both. The important thing is that you make a list with the names of everyone who sits on the committee(s) you want to target. It doesn't matter which chamber those legislators sit in because your bill will have to pass both houses (with the exact same language)—assuming that you're lobbying a body that has two chambers. If so, just choose a starting place and map both sides.

Once you do that, if you look at the websites for your elected officials, you'll find them to be chockfull of information about their interests, accomplishments, and careers. You'll also learn about the organizations they are members of and other committees they sit on. Pay attention to what they do (or did) to earn a living outside of being a legislator. Do they have a family? If so, what does that family look like? Are they a same-sex couple? Do they have pets? Are they a multigenerational family? Do they foster children, or have they adopted children? Those details will give you a clue about whether that legislator might be more or less inclined to support your issue. For those people who were elected more recently, you can look up articles that detail the key issues they talked about during their election campaigns. All those clues will help your group determine who is likely to lend a hand (or oppose your idea).

While you're on a clue-finding hunt about your legislative targets, don't forget to keep an eye out for other legislation they're sponsoring. For example, if your target legislator is laser focused on passing bills having to do with Topic X, that person might not be at all receptive to sponsoring your bill. Also, keep in mind where everyone is in the election cycle. If your idea is controversial, it may not be the right time for that person to raise it.

IT'S A SMALL WORLD

The world is a surprisingly small place. It's likely that if you ask around, you'll find connections to legislators through everyday people you know. You might find that your brother-in-law works at the same company as one of the legislators, a cousin of yours played on the dude's high school football team, or your sister's kids are in the same class as the legislator's kids. These personal connections really do help. After all, legislators are people, too.

When you map out the legislative terrain, it's also critically important to be aware of how each "half" of the legislature plays with the other. The reason I put the word *half* in quotes is because sometimes there is a partisan divide between each house, where Republicans make up most of the members of one side and Democrats the other. Sometimes you have a single house, like a town council or county board, that's also divided by partisanship.

If there is a bitter partisan divide, you'll want to draw upon the personal connections you've discovered in the mapping process to help pave a smooth path for the different parties to work together. Tip O'Neill, a long-time Speaker of the House in Congress, famously said, "All politics is local," by which he meant making personal connections between politicians and constituents is the best way to get things done.[i] Interestingly, he had an extremely close relationship with President Ronald Reagan, who was a member of the opposite party and often held radically different views from Tip. Although you don't see much of that on the national level today, bills that have bipartisan support (meaning, they're sponsored by members of both major parties) are more likely to pass.

HOW THEY DID IT

Gathering support for your cause is essential. What starts out as a few people looking to make a change in their community (or state) turns into a whole lot of people and organizations that share your sentiment.

When you map out your potential supporters, you'll have to be creative and think outside of the box. It is all about finding commonality. For us, we started out by targeting organizations that addressed drug abuse. Some of these organizations specifically focused on minors, which was even better for our purposes. Next, we looked for organizations in health care and education. We initially mapped out local San Diego organizations and gradually expanded our search until we found potential supporters across the state and even some on the national level. While national organizations are great, state legislators largely think locally: "Who supports this *here*?"

Once you've thought about your potential supporters, divide and conquer. Make a list of their names and contact information, including phone number, e-mail, or even Twitter handle, to make it easy for people in your group to contact them. While you're in the process of hunting down their contact info, see if you can identify one or two staff people in key roles and add their direct contact information to your lists. Assign an individual in your group to be the "point person" for each organization you want to recruit. After all, "Many hands make light work." Our group found that an added bonus of contacting potential supporters was that they often directed us to new supporters we hadn't even considered or didn't know existed!

While you might have the feeling that what you are doing is great and there are no downsides, some people or organizations may beg to differ. In mapping out your detractors, it is important to be *completely honest* with yourselves about who might be opposed to your campaign. In many cases, you might not know whether to add an organization to your list of supporters or opposers until you've had a chance to do more research on them. As you do this research, remember that it's important to find out exactly why others are opposed to something that you strongly believe could improve or even save lives. Understanding the why will give you a shot at reframing your arguments to address their concerns and/or develop a joint solution to solving the problem.

Our detractors were big ones: trade associations representing grocery retailers and drug stores. If you asked almost anyone who worked for one of those organizations whether they thought minors should have easy access to DXM to get high, they would surely agree that it was a bad idea; however, organizations aren't people. For those organizations, our proposal to prevent the sale of DXM to minors raised red flags. They were worried about their members being legally liable for deaths caused by products they sold, about those businesses having to train their clerks, about the time those clerks would spend checking IDs, about having to enforce the law, and other similar things. We also discovered that the union representing retail workers did not support our cause because they were afraid a new law could result in workers losing their jobs and/or being held personally liable.

Another big organization *did* prove to be very helpful. While the Consumer Healthcare Products Association (CHPA) said they could not formally endorse our campaign, they did say

continued from previous page

that they supported age restrictions for the sale of DXM and offered to work directly with us to advocate for the legislation. Staff from CHPA provided valuable information about the prior attempt to regulate DXM in our own state as well as efforts to pass laws in other states. They reviewed our white paper and suggested important edits.

However, given that some very influential organizations had serious misgivings about our proposal, we couldn't simply argue that making DXM less accessible to minors outweighed their concerns—especially the issue of legal liability. We took a closer look at our proposed solutions and developed new ones. Originally, we thought it would be a good idea to not have DXM products as accessible in stores, similar to cigarettes. We thought this would help prevent theft of DXM products by minors, but this was too big of a hurdle to jump through to get done. We instead settled on requiring proof of age (18 and over) in order to purchase DXM products.

We also shared our research and information with elected officials so that they knew we had done homework and considered all sides. It makes sense: When bills are drafted, the chances of them being successful will increase if some of the opposition's concerns are addressed upfront. The key lesson here? Connecting with the opposition was just as important as building up our list of supporters!

Ideally, you will continue adding new supporters to your list throughout your campaign, as we did. We also uncovered some interesting surprises along the way that helped us build an even stronger case and find an author for our bill.

One helpful discovery, which we told you about in Chapter 4, was when we found out that we weren't the first people in our state to try to solve this same problem! Seven years earlier, two police officers in Northern California had entered a local "There Oughta Be a Law" contest and proposed a similar idea. If our state had been able to pass a law restricting the sale of DXM back then, there would have been at least one more barrier already in place that could have made it more difficult for young teens (including Annamarie's son) to abuse DXM. It only took a little more research to find out which organizations had supported and opposed this first attempt at passing a new law and then add them to our map.

REFERENCE

i. O'Neill, T., & Hymel, G. (1994). *All politics is local, and other rules of the game*. Crown.

Chapter 8

Step 6: Form a Coalition

Forming a coalition is a natural outgrowth of the mapping process. And if you've ever played or watched any type of team sport, you'll have a good understanding of how coalitions work. On one end of the spectrum are star players out front doing the heavy lifting game after game; on the other end are team members who spend most of their time warming the bench. When you think about it, everyone—no matter what their position—is proud to wear the uniform and be part of the effort. That includes the fans who are cheering from the sidelines decked out in the team's colors.

Like a sports team, building an effective advocacy coalition requires strategy to put together a winning roster, which is what we'll explore in this chapter.

HOW IT'S DONE

Three things I've mentioned in previous chapters about forming a lobbying coalition are worth repeating and exploring in greater detail:

1. Whenever possible, include odd bedfellows.
2. Be sure to enlist people who live or work in the district of the legislators you intend to lobby.
3. Make a solid game plan for how the work will get done.

OPPOSITES ATTRACT!

Sadly, it's almost unimaginable that Democrats and Republicans at all levels of government used to see each other as anything other than warring factions, but they did (and sometimes even married one another!). Legislators used to frequently cross party lines to collaborate on writing and passing legislation that benefitted people who were affected by that issue. Crafting laws shouldn't be about hostage taking, or even horse-trading; it should only be about addressing problems that people face in our society—regardless of political party or religious beliefs, whether they live in a rural area or a big city, etc. The more broad-based your coalition is, the more likely your members will be to connect with legislators who have equally wide-ranging views and political allegiances. That will naturally increase the chances of your bill becoming a law.

This is still true even if, for instance, your state or local legislature happens to be dominated by one party. After all, not all Republicans or Democrats think alike, never mind those who are independent, Green, or Libertarian! As a case in point, you can have Democrats who support the death penalty, who oppose the death penalty, and who favor the death penalty but only if it's administered in a certain way for select types of crimes.

The important thing is to make sure that your coalition has people and organizations in it that can speak directly to politicians who share their worldview and have shared life experiences (ideally, related to your campaign). If you think about it, it's human nature. As sympathetic as we might be to an issue, our sympathies increase if there are people just like us who are backing that issue or who have been directly affected by it. We all gravitate to people we can relate to.

A terrific example of this are alliances that have formed between suicide prevention advocates and proponents of gun rights. Most folks—including many gun owners—are shocked to learn that there are almost twice as many gun deaths by suicide than by homicide (in 2019, the nationwide figure was 23,941 gun suicides[i] vs. 14,414 gun homicides[ii]). To stem the tide, public health professionals across the country reached out to firearms retailers, gun-range owners, and gun-lobby trade associations to talk about these dynamics and to enlist them as partners in their work.

Chuck Aposhian, chair of a Utah gun-owners lobbying group, was one of those people. When he learned that 85% of gun deaths in his state were suicides, he was stunned and motivated to act. As a result, he played a major role in helping to craft laws designed to prevent suicides. Similar efforts have been undertaken in New Hampshire, Washington State, and other places across the country.[iii] You can imagine how powerful it is for a legislator to walk into a meeting with a gun-rights advocate and a public health advocate who are united in their desire to make change.

IT'S LIKE LOVE IN TENNIS

Love is a powerful word that can be used in many ways. The love you have for a parent or spouse isn't anything like the love you have for your favorite brand of peanut butter. If you've ever played tennis, you know that love in tennis means zero. If you don't have members of your coalition who both live and are registered to vote in the districts of the legislators your group is lobbying, you haven't got game. Sure, legislators are public servants—it's just that they care principally about the people they were elected to serve, and those are the people who live in their district (and can vote them in or out of office).

DIVVYING UP THE WORK

If I were a betting woman, I'd wager that when you started thinking about your campaign, the idea took off when you and a few others began to talk passionately about how important it was to create or change a law to address what you perceived to be a huge problem or a tremendous opportunity. At this point, though, you've realized that launching a full-on lobbying campaign is a boatload of work, and that you'll be better off if you can recruit other committed people to help.

As you begin to put together a campaign, you and the members of your group will talk to more and more people about the issue. Some of the new folks you engage will feel equally impassioned by the idea and will spend many hours working with you to mastermind and coordinate the campaign. On the other end, some might be willing to pick up an important but discrete task along the way. Here is a list of some of the tasks that you'll need to divvy up among individual people or small teams:

- Doing background research.
- Writing up the research in a user-friendly format for the fact sheet.
- Designing a logo and formatting the fact sheet.
- Creating a white paper with detailed information on the issue.
- Being a topic expert because that person has direct experience with the issue.
- Putting together a website and social media platform for the campaign.
- Persuading other people and organizations to sign on with the campaign.

- Organizing a public education event or two to spread the word.
- Developing talking points for the media and for your supporters.
- Mobilizing people who live in a particular community or belong to an organization to act.
- Visiting legislators to persuade them to take action by sponsoring or supporting your bill.
- Making sure your group, if it's a formally incorporated nonprofit, is in compliance with the city, county, or state regulations regarding lobbying.

The important thing to realize is that no matter how passionate you are about your cause, you can't do it alone. A simple thing to keep in mind when you do outreach is this: People who have been directly affected by the issue, or who will feel the impact of the law if it's passed, will be much more likely to roll up their sleeves to help your campaign. Each of your coalition members will play a different role helping you move the ball down the field, depending upon their time and interest in the issue. *Don't be distraught if everyone isn't doing an equal amount of work.* Do devise a plan of action that minimally identifies the following:

1. Who in the group will chart out a rough timeline for the campaign and the steps that need to be done along the way? When is the first opportunity for a bill to be introduced? After you know that, you can work backward to determine how much time you'll need to convince someone to carry your bill, who that person might be (based upon the mapping work you did in Step 5), and what materials you'll need to show that person (and the others you'll lobby) to persuade them to adopt your cause. Since those lobbying campaign materials will include a list of coalition members who have signed on to your campaign, you can see how one thing builds on the next.

2. Who are the core members of the campaign (you can also call yourself the "steering committee") and what decisions will that group be entrusted to make as you move along?

How will that group and the larger coalition make decisions: by a majority vote or by consensus? If you are voting, does each member have an equal vote, or do organizations that represent a greater number of people who are affected by the issue have more voting power? As new members of your coalition are added, what decision-making powers will they have? For instance, who gets to vote on the name of your campaign, and later on, as your campaign advances, who gets to decide whether your group agrees with changes that legislators propose making to your bill?

3. Which organizations and individuals will be responsible for each step in the process?

Who will hold them accountable for following through on their commitments? Does the work done in subcommittees need to be ultimately approved by the core campaign group?

4. Who is the primary point person(s) that policymakers and their aides speak to when they have questions about your issue?

[You'll want to identify one or two people who can be relied upon to respond quickly and accurately with any questions that arise.

5. Who is entrusted to speak to the media?

If you are clear from the beginning about who is responsible for what, you will minimize feelings of resentment along the lines of "so-and-so thinks she's 'all that' and in charge" while "what's-his-name isn't doing 'jack' like the rest of us." You might also have a coalition member who happens to have a long-term friendship with one of your key legislators, and that member's only role is to call that legislator to put in a good word for your bill idea. In fact, coalition members that have long-term relationships with legislators fare best.

Whatever you do, please make sure that *each and every* coalition member has signed on to your campaign in writing and understands *exactly* what that means. You want to be absolutely sure, beyond a shadow of a doubt, that your fact sheet lists only those people and organizations that have officially agreed to back your cause. The last thing in the world you need is for any individual or group to claim that you are using their names without permission. That type of charge could potentially undermine all your work. Similarly, if you get to a point where one or more members of your coalition want to resign because they or their organizations don't agree with your tactics or shift in position, please take the time to listen to their concerns and, if no resolution can be found, graciously allow their organization to back out. You want to have people and organizations behind you who have no reservations about what you are trying to accomplish and how you are conducting your campaign.

HOW THEY DID IT

Once we had mapped out a good number of potential supporters, it was time to get them on board our campaign! The thought of contacting people might give you cold feet if the list of names on your roster are people you've never met (let's be honest, no one likes cold calling). If you're feeling anxious about reaching out to them by phone, try sending an e-mail or messaging them on Twitter. While a phone call has the benefit of getting in touch with someone in real time, online messaging is arguably just as

---

beneficial. Sending an e-mail adds the perk of quickly attaching relevant materials, like your fact sheet, that might give individuals and organizations a good reason to join your cause.

When we formed our coalition, we started with local contacts and then expanded to state and national organizations. We liked this strategy for two reasons. First, it was easier to get people and organizations on the local level to sign onto our cause because, by using our network, we could almost always find someone who was connected to them. Second, the more coalition members we had, the easier it was to get new members to sign on when they saw the list of other people and organizations who had already joined our campaign.

During the recruitment process we also learned that social media was our friend. Using Twitter was a great strategy for adding new members, especially for recruiting organizations beyond the local level. Twitter was not only good when we started our mapping phase, it was also helpful for directly contacting organizations about joining our coalition.

We quickly realized that building a coalition would be an ongoing activity throughout our campaign. The initial map of potential supporters we created in Step 5 was just a starting point. As we reached out to new people, they often suggested contacts at other organizations or individuals who were not on our original list. This meant that we needed to make frequent updates to the names of people and organizations who supported us on all of the materials we distributed or posted online. As the list kept expanding, we made sure to have the most up-to-date list printed on any materials that we brought to meetings with state legislators.

One area we struggled with during this phase was finding more organizations to join our coalition that were based in other

continued from previous page

legislative districts throughout the state whose legislators we identified during our mapping phase and planned to lobby. We still managed to get initial meetings with these legislators when we were looking for a sponsor for our bill, but more coalition members might have helped us get even more legislators on board. At the end of the day, the legislators serve their constituents above everyone else. While we were still successful with our campaign, it's easy to see the benefits of having more geographically diverse supporters throughout various legislative districts in order to gain widespread support for future causes.

When we started meeting with legislators to find an author for our bill, we only had a few fully confirmed organizations and prominent individuals signed on with our campaign. Most of our coalition members were local San Diego groups that dealt with drug abuse prevention (thankfully, one was a children's hospital, which added a lot of clout). Eventually, we added three state organizations to our list. Some we persuaded to join after just a call or two, while others required multiple conversations and e-mails. Altogether, we had 12 confirmed and pending coalition members when we made our first visit to our state capital for meetings with legislators.

Asking members to join our coalition was not just about getting them to "sign on" initially so that we could list their names on our campaign materials. After we nailed down an author for our bill, we needed them to be active participants in promoting the campaign by contacting their local elected officials directly and asking them to support the bill. Because most people are so busy these days, we knew that their good intentions might not yield results unless we made it *very* easy for them to help. We drafted a "sample letter" for each new coalition member with instructions to use it as a starting point for contacting their legislators. (See figure 8.1 at the end of this chapter). Often, people used these drafts without making any significant changes, but we took extra time to personalize each letter by adding the legislator's name and address to each sample. We also included the name, phone number, and e-mail address for that person's legislative aide to make it even easier for our coalition members to follow up. Our goal was for each of our coalition members to get their legislator to send a letter of support to our bill's author. Someone in our group then followed up to make sure that these letters to legislators were requested, collected, and eventually sent to the author of our bill.

Looking back, approaching more local and state law enforcement agencies to join our coalition was a missed opportunity. The senator who authored our bill was someone who had first been introduced to the dangers associated with DXM abuse by concerned police officers in his district. It's likely that police officers in other districts were already aware of the situation and may have helped elevate the urgency of our case in the eyes of more state legislators. Another way we could have strengthened our coalition would have been to encourage all of our members to help us invite additional members to join. This certainly would have increased our total membership and put added pressure on legislators throughout the state.

As we told you at the beginning of our story, our campaign began during an advocacy course taught by Pat, when a core group of four people who did not know one another formed a group to work on this project. Throughout the campaign, we focused on

continued from previous page

dividing up responsibilities and helping each other stay on task to complete each step. Frequent meetings, phone calls, e-mail exchanges, and a master calendar (updated regularly) kept everyone in our group up-to-date. The fact that we had different backgrounds and political beliefs proved very helpful, especially as we began recruiting coalition members, and even more so when we began contacting and meeting with legislators.

REFERENCES

i.   Centers for Disease Control and Prevention. (2021). *FastStats: Suicide and self-harm injury.* Retrieved September 15, 2021 from https://www.cdc.gov/nchs/fastats/suicide.htm

ii. Centers for Disease Control and Prevention. (2021). *FastStats: Assault or Homicide.* Retrieved September 15, 2021, from https://www.cdc.gov/nchs/fastats/homicide.htm

iii. Roni Caryn Rabin. (2020, November 17). 'How did we not know?' Gun owners confront a suicide epidemic. *The New York Times.* Retrieved September 15, 2021, from https://www.nytimes.com/2020/11/17/health/suicide-guns-prevention.html

Senator Loni Hancock
Chair, Public Safety Committee
California State Capitol, Rm. 2031
Sacramento, CA 95814

Re: Senate Bill 514 (SUPPORT)

Dear Senator Hancock,

As my state representative, I seek your help with supporting Senate Bill 514; NO COST legislation to stop the sale of cough medicine containing Dextromethorphan (DXM) to minors. DXM is the most commonly used cough suppressant drug and is found in over 140 over-the-counter cough and cold medicines. Because it is legal, inexpensive and easily accessible, teenagers are using and abusing DXM to get high without understanding the side effects of overdosing.

Annually, more than 400,000 Californians, ages 11–17, abuse DXM to get high. Overdose can cause seizures, coma, brain damage and can kill a first time user. According to the Drug Abuse Warning Network, emergency room visits related to DXM abuse rose 70% between 2004–2007; this problem is real.

Teens who abuse DXM believe it's a "safe high" because its legal and easily available in the same stores that sell gum and soda.

Figure 8.1 Sample Letter

DXM is a synthetically produced substance that is chemically related to codeine, though it is not an opiate. DXM is used in over-the-counter medicines to raise the coughing threshold of the brain and has replaced codeine as the most widely used cough suppressant in the United States. It is available in capsule, liquid, liquid gelatin capsule, lozenge, and tablet forms.

California can take the lead on this critical issue to protect minors with ZERO COST to the State. The state of California will not be faced with additional financial burden because fines incurred by commercial establishments will pay for any costs of enforcement. California can be a leader in ending DXM abuse. The proposed legislation will save teens lives with NO COST to the state of California.

As your constituent (or AS AN ORGANIZATION THAT CARES DEEPLY ABOUT THE WELL BEING OF CHILDREN), I urge you to support S 514 which will require an 18 and over ID for the purchase of cough medicine containing DXM.

Sincerely,

Name or Organization
Address

Cc: Senator Joe Simitian

Chapter 9

Step 7: Develop Educational Materials

Developing easy-to-use, action-focused educational materials—and sharing them with people you want to activate in your networks— is your *Make Way for Ducklings* moment. If you've never been to Boston or read the children's book, it's the story of a family of ducks who can't get home without the aid of friendly police officers who help them cross several busy roads. For this step in the process, you're going to rally all of your ducklings to contact friendly public officials who will work with you to move your issue along. It's one of the easiest steps, and it draws upon many of the other things you've already done. For that reason, some of the content in this chapter may seem like songs I've already sung; however, try think of it as a chorus and get in the groove with me.

In Step 3, you created a fact sheet, which you branded in Step 4, that brilliantly summarizes your campaign issue so that anyone who is remotely interested in the topic can understand the situation and your proposal for addressing it. In Steps 5 and 6, you dedicated brainpower and people power to identifying allies and recruiting them to join you. Step 7 involves giving everyone in your network easy-to-understand information and marching orders (or, if you prefer, waddling orders) that show them how to engage with legislators in various ways.

HOW IT'S DONE

Ideally, many members of your coalition are organizations that have active members or are connected to networks of people in their communities or fields. Your job is to figure out how to energize as many of these folks as possible to weigh in on your side and to make sure they spin the issue the way you want it spun. The math is simple: The more people you can convince to take action on your issue by contacting their elected officials in an effective and appropriate way, the more success you'll have persuading those officials to do something. This is where your mobilization and education work comes in.

Taking inventory of your coalition's assets involves making some estimates about how many people your coalition can get to:

- Send emails to legislators.
- Write postcards.
- Call legislators.
- Do outreach to other folks and organizations that may be interested in the issue so that they generate e-mails and phone calls to legislators.
- Write letters to the editor about the issue.
- Visit legislators to talk about the issue.

If you're working on a neighborhood issue, you might also want to have a group gather signatures on a petition.

The trick is to coordinate these activities, shape the messaging, and if possible, keep track of how many people are doing which types of things. You'll want to activate your member organizations to do the following four things:

1. Hold an education session on the issue for members of their organization/community.

The advantage of having a question-and-answer session rather than just sending folks e-mails describing the issue is that, well, it allows them to ask questions and to get answers to those questions. That helps them become better informed and, hopefully, more enthusiastic about taking some type of action that will advance your cause. If it's easier, you can also sponsor issue education sessions that anyone affiliated with one of your coalition partners can attend, but know that the more personal the invitation, the more likely folks are to show up. In other words, the invitation to the event needs to come from the member organization, not from your group.

2. Distribute "dummies" guides to your issue.

Of course, not everyone who belongs to those organizations will attend an educational event. To reach those folks who don't, you'll want your member organizations to circulate simple-to-understand nuggets of information about your issue—bite-sized pieces of your fact sheet, including testimonials from people who have been affected by it—that quickly educate their people about the issue, why it's important to act, and how they can become involved in the campaign.

3. Send out "how-to" materials to their members (and keep track of how many respond).

When the time is right, your campaign will want to generate postcards, e-mails, and phone calls to legislators (or, again, circulate a petition if you are working on a neighborhood issue). To do any of those things well, you need to make it *easy* for folks to participate because most of them will not be as fired up about the issue as you are. Many will want to be supportive of it, but only if it doesn't take up too much of their time. If you want people to take action, you've got to sketch out a brief set of *talking points* that they can use to help shape their message. You'll also need to provide links containing the snail mail addresses, e-mail addresses, and telephone numbers for legislators that will enable people to do the task in *under a minute* (or something close to that).

The most important thing for everyone to understand and be trained on is that politicians and their proxies care about the *way* their constituents communicate with them. If legislators receive an avalanche of postcards or e-mails or calls about a particular issue but all those postcards, e-mails, and calls are the same, word for word, that's like being bombarded with a tidal wave of junk. It's not nearly as good as a smaller number of personalized postcards, e-mails, or telephone calls that talk about different reasons why the issue matters. There are two important rules here: 1) The more personalized the interaction, the more it counts, and 2) *all* messages must be polite and appropriate. In my time on the planet, I've never met a human being who responded positively to being threatened or called a f@*&king a$$h@le or anything similar. Politicians are no different.

Sometimes organizations like to combine brief issue training with phone banks or postcard writing parties. That can help attract people who like to work as part of a team.

You'll also want to ask the advocates who are part of your member organizations to sign up for regular alerts that they'll receive by e-mail, text, or tweet about what new action they can take as the issue moves through the process.

4. Identify a core group of their members who are dedicated to the issue.

If possible, you'll want each of your allied organizations to identify two types of people who will work on the campaign.

One set will be dedicated worker-bees who will agree to be trained on the issue so that they can reach out to other organizations and people to spread the word, urge them to act, and provide training or links to the resources you've created for this purpose. This group could also be deployed to get signatures on a petition, but know that petitions aren't nearly as persuasive as the other things I've mentioned, simply because they require less effort on the part of the person signing.

The other set will be people who are willing to meet with legislators. Depending on your issue, it's ideal if many of these folks have experienced it first-hand. You'll want to spend some time rehearsing for these meetings to make sure that everyone is comfortable telling their story, can do so in a way that's compelling and easy to follow, and has the same talking points about the solution to the problem. Rehearsing is key. More than once, I've seen beads of sweat pop out on the brows of some very experienced community leaders when they've met with elected officials on issues that are important to them.

WHY IS ALL OF THIS NECESSARY?

The truth is that lawmakers really do care when their constituents contact them (and *constituents* in this sense means people who live in or own businesses in their districts and *vote*). And yes, they really do check to see if people who contact them about a particular issue are *registered* to vote. The reason they care is because if their constituents are happy with their job performance, those folks will go to the polls and reelect them. It doesn't matter if those being lobbied are legislators or their aides—someone will check to see if you are registered to vote. After all, their job security depends upon whether the elected official stays in office. Staff people, no matter how high up they are on the food chain, act as a proxy for the elected person.

For instance, if I am an aide to a city council member or legislator and I don't listen to what the people in my district want (or, for that matter, don't listen politely), then they won't be happy with my boss, they'll express their unhappiness by voting for our opponent, and I'll soon find myself stocking shelves. You would think the one exception to this rule is when the politician is a lame duck, meaning that person either can't run for office again because the law forbids it (due to term limits) or just doesn't want to run again. But most politicians really do want to serve the greater good and sincerely care when people in their communities take the time to contact them about an issue, regardless of how long they have been or will continue to stay in office.

The biggest impact is when constituents take the time to schedule a visit with officials or their proxies to discuss the issue face to face. Sure, you can always try to drop in unannounced, but scheduled visits work much more effectively. What advocates I've worked with have found to be most surprising when they meet legislators or their aides for the first time is how willing those folks are to listen to the issue being presented. Honestly, it makes me more than a little sad that people are astonished by this phenomenon because that's what these policymakers get paid to do—to serve the people.

Of course, part of this lovefest has to do with how much thought and preparation has gone into the presentation. You can be as impressive as the most well-paid lobbyist if you are able to calmly talk through your issue, clearly present the research you've done (summarized on your fact sheet), and answer any and all questions they might raise. You'll want to rehearse with everyone in your group in advance—that includes your team and anyone else who you've brought along to speak directly about their experience. Public officials are always impressed when citizens take the time to speak to them in person (and even more so if folks have to travel for that purpose). That matters because it shows how much you and your colleagues care about your issue.

If you live in or near your state capital or are lobbying for a cause that has to do with county or city government, it's pretty easy to set up some face time with the policy makers or their proxies. Chapter 11 shares some ideas about the best ways to approach them.

To be frank, though, even if you live close by, most of *your* constituents—that is, those people you know who are most affected by the issue—won't go to an in-person meeting. They won't go for a variety of reasons: Some have full-time jobs and can't get off work; others have difficulty getting around because they're frail and it's cold, or they have kids to look after, or whatever. Some might be scared or embarrassed to speak publicly about the issue. It's really OK—actually, it's more than OK—if you don't have a hoard of people at your visit with legislators as long as you have people who know what they're talking about and are all on the same page with your campaign. The fact sheet listing your coalition members will show that you have strength in numbers. Going back to our odd bedfellows, you'll ideally want to have people from a variety of organizations playing similar roles so that everyone who's meeting with an office holder doesn't come from the same type of organization (think back to our gun rights and suicide prevention advocates working as a team).

The total number of all those people who are willing to act on behalf of your issue is of bottom-line importance. You want to be able to say to the people you are lobbying that your group represents so many concerned citizens.

HOW THEY DID IT

At this point, we were full steam ahead! We had grown our coalition, and it was time to put them to work! While it was great to be able to list all our coalition members on our website and various materials to demonstrate how many organizations were committed to our campaign, we knew this was not the only role they could play.

Coalition members can and should be used to promote your cause. However, it is up to you to motivate them to get involved and to help them do it quickly, easily, and effectively. At the end of this chapter are a few examples of our outreach efforts and education efforts that we hope did just that. After all, what's better than making a big impact? Making a big impact and doing it without a lot of effort.

COVER SHEET

18 and Over the Counter

Write to your legislator! Stop the sale of cough medicine to minors!!

Products containing DXM (**Dextromethorphan**) are legal over the counter drugs: visible, inexpensive and easily accessible to teenagers. Annually, more than 400,000 Californians, ages 11–17, abuse DXM to get high. Overdose can cause seizures, coma, brain damage and can kill a first-time user!

We are trying to pass legislation that will ban the sale of cough medicines containing DXM to minors. It is critical that California Legislators understand the danger of cough medicine abuse teens are involved in and the danger it poses to the youth of our state!!

Legislators can support this measure by co-sponsoring the bill to the state assembly. Urge them to support this bill!!

The following is a letter you can use to help facilitate your contact to your legislator. Feel free to modify as you like to include how you feel about this issue personally and protecting the youth of our state.

Figure 9.1 Cover Sheet

Sample letter to Legislator

Dear XXXX,

As my state representative, I am seeking your help in supporting a bill to stop the sale of cough medicine to minors. Products containing DXM (**Dextromethorphan**) are legal over the counter drugs: visible, inexpensive and easily accessible to teenagers.

Annually, more than 400,000 Californians, ages 11–17, abuse DXM to get high. Overdose can cause seizures, coma, brain damage and can kill a first-time user!

Teens who abuse DXM believe it's a "safe high" because it's legal and easily available in the same stores that sell gum and soda.

DXM is a synthetically produced substance that is chemically related to codeine, though it is not an opiate. DXM is used in over-the-counter medicines to raise the coughing threshold of the brain and has replaced codeine as the most widely used cough suppressant in the United States. It is available in capsule, liquid, liquid gelatin capsule, lozenge, and tablet forms.

California can be a leader in this type of legislation to protect our youth! The state of California will not be faced with additional financial burden because fines incurred by commercial establishments will pay for any costs of enforcement.

As your constituent, I urge you to support legislation banning the sale of cough medicine to minors.

Sincerely,

Your Name

Talking Points for "18 and Over the Counter" Supporters:

- 18 and Over-the-Counter is an advocacy campaign to stop the sales of Dextromethorphan (DXM) to minors in California.
- DXM is an active ingredient in more than 140 cough and cold medicines.
- Products containing DXM are legal over the counter drugs: visible, inexpensive and easily accessible to teenagers.
- *Annually, more than 400,000 Californians, ages 11–17, abuse DXM to get high.*

- *Overdose can cause seizures, coma, brain damage and can kill a first time user*
- Teens who abuse DXM believe it's a "safe high" because it's legal and easily available in the same stores that sell gum and soda.
- Street names include: Skittles, Robo, Tussin, Velvet, Triple-C, Vitamin D, Red-Devils imply light-hearted, candy-like fun.
- Teens don't know that the dangers multiply when DXM is abused with alcohol, prescription drugs or narcotics.
- DXM is a synthetically produced substance that is chemically related to codeine, though it is not an opiate. DXM is used in over-the-counter medicines to raise the coughing threshold of the brain and has replaced codeine as the most widely used cough suppressant in the United States. It is available in capsule, liquid, liquid gelatin capsule, lozenge, and tablet forms.
- California can be a leader in ending DXM abuse. The proposed legislation will save teens lives with NO COST to the state of California.
- Local government and law enforcement will be reimbursed with funds collected through fines:
  - Stores violating the age limits will be fined no more than $200 for the first offense, $500 for the second offense and $1,000 per subsequent offense.

Chapter 10

Step 8: Launch a Media Campaign

Once upon a time, we lived in a rosy media land where everyone got their news from the same source—either their local paper or one of three TV networks that presented an evening news show. The country was less divided then because Americans consumed the same information. Today, it's a whole different ballgame. We get news through our own screens, and what we pick up depends on which sources we're following. That makes the job of launching a media campaign for your issue a little more complicated than it might first appear. This chapter covers how to use both social media and mainstream media to attract attention to your issue (things that often intersect when articles and commentary from mainstream reporters are shared online).

HOW IT'S DONE

I'm going to start with social media. Social media strategy is like dog food. What I mean by that is this: All the dogs I've ever owned have loved to eat, and every one of them has informed me in their own way that I don't feed them enough (for the record, this isn't true). When I give my dog Miles a bowl of food, it's gone before I can blink. If I were to give Miles an open bag of kibble, chances are the situation would get crazy very quickly. Similarly, the thing to remember about social media is that it's chockfull of wonderful tools that, if used well, will work to your advantage. At the same time, you need to do everything possible to control it—especially the messaging for your campaign—and to do that, you'll want to be sure to assign someone (or a team of someones) to coordinate it. I don't need to tell you how easily things can turn into an open bag of dog food.

It all starts with your website, which is the baseline of what you'll need. Your website will explain your issue (outlining the problem and the solution), offer testimonials (written statements or videos of people who have been affected by your issue), list who is on board your campaign, convey where you are in the lobbying process (for example, we're meeting with city councilmember Soledad Delgado next week to present our proposal to her, or Representative Darrel Jackson has agreed to sponsor our bill!), and give instructions for what you want the reader to do next (fear not! I'll cover this in Chapters 11 and 12).

The what-to-do-next instructions on your website are where all of those talking points you developed in Step 7 (see Chapter 9) come into play. Those obviously need to be posted and updated as your bill (hopefully) moves through the process. You'll of course want to post your position paper and, if possible, provide links to a Facebook page, YouTube or TikTok videos (if you have any), and/or your Twitter feed. I'm not a fan of online petitions because research shows that they're not very effective.[i] It makes sense that since they're so easy to create, they wouldn't have a big impact on lawmakers. But if you or someone in your group is set on doing one, go for it.

In addition to all of that, you'll want to be sure to have a way for people to sign up to receive e-mail messages or text alerts about the campaign. That way, you can mobilize them to take action at critical points in the lobbying process. You can also put a donation link on your website, but unless you have a lot of travel expenses because you live far from your state capital, or need to pay for someone to coordinate your campaign and website, this is probably unnecessary. There are, of course, lots of other fancy things you can do if you have access to tech-savvy people, like put interactive maps on your website or use virtual reality to show people what the problem looks like, but I find that for most grassroots campaigns, a simple website works just fine.

Needless to say, but I'm going to say it anyway, the information on your website, along with all of the other materials you produce for your campaign, needs to be accurate and consistent. A big part of controlling the messaging is making triple sure that:

- You have checked all your facts.
- All your listed supporters have actually signed on to your campaign.
- The spokespeople who have been affected by your issue are of good character and able to speak clearly about the issue.
- Those speakers are prepared to field some potentially ugly questions (this is yucky, I know, but it can happen).
- You through your website and your speakers through their voices repeat the same clear message over and over and over and over.

TRADITIONAL MEDIA COVERAGE

There are two primary reasons why you want to get traditional media coverage of your issue, and they feed off one another. First, the more people who know about your issue, the more likely you'll find some who will do something to support your effort. If you're lucky, you might attract a few people who are interested in joining your campaign, but your biggest hope is finding folks who are moved to call their elected official and say, "I read an article (or heard a story on the radio) about X and feel strongly that the law needs to be changed/created." Second, the more traditional news coverage you get, the more likely policymakers will be to pay attention to your cause. Mainstream media does add a stamp of legitimacy, and legislators know that the reach of those outlets can translate into both public support for an issue and increased scrutiny of their actions.

What works particularly well is if you can include a news story as part of the packet of materials you'll bring to your meeting with legislators (or their aides, or other policymakers—in other words, whomever you're lobbying). Seeing your cause reported in the press makes it seem like a big deal, and it is because through the media, you've been able to convey your message to a broader group of people. If you can get a photo of your issue, that's an added bonus. Best of all, if you time things just right, you can get the story to appear within a week of your visits to legislators and their aides. Getting radio and TV coverage is also good in terms of spreading the word, but ideally, you want to have something you can print out and bring to a meeting.

If you've never done any of this, where do you begin? Jeff McDonald, an investigative reporter at *The San Diego Union-Tribune*, has given me and other advocates lots of great advice on how to deal with the media. Here are some of his tips that I've learned over the years:

1. **Identify and reach out to reporters at local media outlets.**
Figure out which news organizations and reporters cover what types of stories. You don't want to pitch a "feel-good" story to an investigative reporter, and you don't want to sell an in-depth story to a columnist who focuses on heartwarming human-interest stories

(unless your campaign is one). Basically, you'll want to identify reporters who write stories on topics that are similar to yours.

Next, find someone in your group who agrees to be the point person for the media. This will be someone who can be called upon to be quoted as an expert on your issue. That person should then reach out to one reporter at each publication you want to target (don't sweat it if it's only one publication) to meet with them along with other members of your group. At the meeting, tell the reporter why your issue matters and the facts (you'll want to give them a copy of your fact sheet and white paper). If they won't meet with you in person, try to set up a time to talk by phone.

You might be disappointed to find that reporters aren't interested in your idea when you first pitch it, but as it gathers steam with community events or at the legislative level, they might change their mind and give it some coverage. For that reason, it's important to keep in contact with reporters you've connected with when important developments happen in your campaign. Also, *always* remember to be polite and professional when speaking with these folks. If you yell at them because they choose not to cover your issue at first, then they'll never cover any story related to your efforts.

2. Write a press release.

If you spend a few minutes online, you'll find lots of sample press releases that you can use as a model for your campaign. The most important elements are to keep it to a single page, provide a quick summary of your issue, list all the members of your coalition, include your website address, and have contact information for your media point person. Jeff always reminds me, "Press releases are 'glorified sales pitches'—they aren't stories. The idea is to 'sell' the reporter on the idea of investigating or covering the story, not to write it."

You'll want to send your press release to specific reporters and, after you send it, follow up with a call to make sure it's been received (but don't hound the reporter!). Remember, it's OK to target multiple media outlets at the same time. If you're sending a press release, they'll know that that's your media strategy. Alternatively, you can target a single reporter at the largest newspaper in your area to offer that person an *exclusive*, which is saying that you are allowing that reporter to cover the story before anyone else. If you decide to go the exclusive route, you cannot ethically send the press release or talk about the story with any other media outlet once the reporter decides to write or otherwise produce your story.

3. **Create an event for your campaign that is designed to attract news coverage.**

You could, for example, call an event to make a public announcement of a study, poll, or other research you've done that highlights the importance of your issue. Use your coalition to turn out people—the larger the crowd, the more newsworthy the event. Remember to involve your entire coalition—the media is more likely to cover your event if more than one organization is hosting it.

4. **When reporters call . . .**

- Make sure you have developed "talking points" in advance so that you are able to "stay on message."
- Be sure to *always tell the truth!* If a reporter asks a question that you don't know the answer to, just admit what you don't know. You can always ask why that particular piece of information is important in the hope that you can answer it with a different fact. If the reporter still isn't satisfied, tell them you'll get back to them once you do have an answer.
- If you want to give a reporter background on the story but you don't want to be quoted on that information, you can say, "This information that I'm about to tell you now is 'off the record.'" For example, you may want to tell the reporter about

someone who has done something so horrible and off the wall against your cause that you want to have it known but don't want to be quoted talking about that person's actions. Just be careful, though, that you have thoroughly checked your facts before going down that path so that the reporter can verify what happened.

• Finally, always be sure to always return a reporter's call as quickly as possible.

Keep in mind that relationships with the media are like relationships with anybody else—it takes time to build trust. Reporters need to know that you're a solid citizen who isn't selling them a bunch of bad information.

HOW THEY DID IT

At this point, our cause was already gaining traction, with new coalition members on board and educational materials developed and sent out. We were ready for our next step: media coverage. There was no outlet too small for us to help move our cause forward. We knew that anything that was published would give us even more confidence going into our meetings with state legislators.

At the end of the chapter is a press release we created for our media campaign. In addition to our press release, we reached out to local news outlets to do a piece on our efforts. We also did our best to be active on social media but primarily used Twitter and Facebook to help promote our issue. If we did it all over again today, we would have been much more active on social

---

media to raise awareness of our issue and would have utilized the numerous social media outlets (Instagram, Facebook, Twitter, TikTok, Snapchat) more effectively. To our credit, however, social media wasn't as prevalent then, and some of the outlets mentioned didn't even exist or were not nearly as popular as they are today.

REFERENCE

i. Elnoshokaty, A. S., Deng, S., & Kwak, D. H. (2016). Success factors of online petitions. In *49th Hawaii International Conference on System Sciences* (pp. 1979–1985). IEEE.

PRESS RELEASE

Contact: NAME

Phone: #

Email: Email

Stop the Sale of Cough Medicine to Minors!!

The advocacy group, "18 and Over the Counter" is traveling to the state capital on Monday, January 10th to find legislative support for a bill to stop the sale of cough medicine to minors.

Members of the group have been leading a grassroots effort to build support for legislation that will protect teens from abusing this over the counter drug. Coalition members will be meeting with Assembly member Toni Atkins on Friday, January 7th to discuss this issue further.

- DXM (Dextromethorphan) is an active ingredient in more than 140 cough and cold medicines.
- Products containing DXM are legal over the counter drugs: visible, inexpensive and easily accessible to teenagers.

Figure 10.1 Press Release

- *Annually, more than 400,000 Californians, ages 11–17, abuse DXM to get high.*
- *Overdose can cause seizures, coma, brain damage and can kill a first time user*
- Teens who abuse DXM believe it's a "safe high" because it's legal and easily available in the same stores that sell gum and soda.

Californians wishing to support this cause can contact **NAME** at **18andOvertheCounter@gmail.com** for more information or send letters to your local and state representatives asking for support. We can help!

Chapter 11

Step 9: Approach Elected Officials

I'm excited just thinking about Step 9. This is the moment you've been waiting for, and you've done a lot of work to get here. You know all about your issue, you've got a nice-looking fact sheet and well-researched position paper, you've given your campaign the best name you could think of, you've built a broad-based coalition, you know who your opposition will be and the arguments they'll probably throw at your idea, and you've rehearsed your spiel along with the other folks who will be lobbying with you.

To get this far, you did a lot of good research in Step 5 (see Chapter 7): learning who chairs and sits on the committees you want to lobby, how many of your coalition members live in the districts your legislative targets represent, and who, if anyone, knows those any of these people on a personal basis. This chapter walks you through how to get an appointment, who should be at the meeting, what to expect, and what to do.

HOW IT'S DONE

Before you pick up the phone to schedule any appointments, you need to check the legislative calendar for the entity (town, city, county, state) you plan to lobby. The calendar should be posted online and easy to read. It will let you know when the legislative body is in session and what the bill-filing deadline is. These facts are important to know: You don't want to schedule a time to meet with legislators when they're not in session, and you don't want to ask them to sponsor a bill on your issue if the filing deadline has passed. It's fine if your group wants to schedule a more informal, get-to-know-you meeting with your legislators for the purpose of telling them about your organization without asking them for anything—just be sure to do it when they're not in the middle of their busy work season.

Once you know the timing is right, call the offices of your elected officials to schedule appointments to meet with them. The background research you did beforehand will allow you to personalize those calls so that you can say something like:

> Hello, my name is Miles Libby. I'm calling on behalf of the HDC—the Hungry Dog Coalition—representing 20,000 canines from across the state. We're planning a trip to the capitol on such and such a date and would like to make an appointment to meet with Representative Stein because he's been such a big supporter of canines, including his own mutt, Schleppy. We'd like to meet with the Representative to discuss some thoughts we have on strengthening animal cruelty prevention laws so that our humans will be required to feed us more kibble.

You will be more likely to get an appointment if, like Miles,[1] you quickly demonstrate your familiarity with the work of the Representative by showing that you know about his efforts to sponsor previous legislation that is related to your cause. If he's a newly elected official, you can draw upon the interests that are stated

---

1. For the record, Miles doesn't speak English (he communicates by barking and whining on occasion). As you know from Chapter 10, this is the issue that he would lobby to address—if he could.

on his website, including those organizations for which he's volunteered (as was discussed for the mapping step in Chapter 7).

While your goal is to set up a time to meet with your elected official, you may be scheduled to meet with that person's designee. Now you might be saying, "Designee?! No way, José. I'm putting a ton of work into this campaign, and I don't want to meet with Representative Singh's legislative assistant—I want to meet with the Representative herself!" Chances are that if the Representative is available when you plan to visit, she may be willing to meet with you—at least for a while and depending on how far you've traveled to see her.

More likely, you'll meet with someone in her office, a legislative aide who is knowledgeable about your topic or other policy areas related to the topic. If you think about this, it makes sense. The legislators you'll be lobbying serve on different committees; they hire staff who are or become experts in those areas.[2] If you do a good job, that staffer will end up being your internal advocate. Being an internal advocate means the aide will keep your issue in the forefront of the Representative's mind, remind her about your key talking points, update her on things like how many new organizations are signing on to your coalition every week, and if you're able to develop a good relationship with the aide, keep you in the loop on various opportunities and obstacles for getting your legislation introduced, sometimes even steering you to another member of the committee who is interested in authoring the bill. Because of all the work they do behind the scenes, meeting with legislative aides is just as important as meeting with lawmakers.

---

2. This can be somewhat different for smaller local governments who share staff. Still, it's always good to get a meeting with whatever legislator or aide you can snag.

The lesson here is not to feel like your campaign is stalled if you can't score an initial meeting with the big cheese. In most cases, you'll find that legislative staff are pretty smart (the higher ranking the office, the more experienced the aides tend to be), and if the elected official is interested in your issue, that staffer will be able to give you tremendous guidance on how to shape your campaign. In fact, when you lobby a branch of government where legislators have term limits, the aides may know more about how the system works than the legislators themselves because they've been in the building longer!

WHO SHOULD BE AT THE MEETING?

Sometimes citizen lobbying groups believe they should show up at a legislator's office with a huge number of people as a way of making a point that they have a lot of support for their issue. This really isn't necessary (and can sometimes be distracting) because you'll be able to show that you have lots of supporters behind you in the form of the organizations you list on your fact sheet that are members of your coalition, and by the e-mails, calls, and postcards you'll generate in support of your issue once you find a legislator to sponsor a bill on your behalf.

So, who needs to be at the meeting? You'll want to have one or two people who are capable of talking about the facts and answering questions in a straightforward way, one or two people who have been affected by the issue and can talk about it from a personal perspective, and several people who represent different types of supporters (your odd bedfellows). Since some of these people will likely play duplicate roles—for instance, someone who has experienced the issue may also be the fact expert—you'll be fine if you have three to five people representing your entire coalition. Just remember that whoever is at the meeting needs to talk about your coalition of supporters and how many individuals that represents (including those voters who live in the legislator's district).

MAKING THE TRIP

If you are working on a county, city, or other local government issue, you'll likely go to those places (city hall or the county seat) to lobby your elected officials. In small states such as Rhode Island, Delaware, Connecticut, New Jersey, or Massachusetts, no one lives that far from the state capitol. In those states, there's really no excuse not to visit your state legislators in their own offices.

If you live far away from the place where your legislators work, then you have several options. Online meetings are becoming increasingly popular. Many people prefer them for the obvious reason that they save time and money. If you decide to go the online route for an initial meeting, I would still recommend that your group form a plan for meeting them later on in person. It's not that different from online dating—it's hard to make a real connection with someone you haven't met in person.

Your legislator will have an office in your district, and you can set up an appointment to meet there. The only problem with that is that the policy people—that is, the legislative aide whose job it is to understand and work on the issues related to your cause—are housed at the state capitol and don't tend to spend much time in the district. You can get lucky at times by developing a good relationship with someone in your local legislator's office who can arrange for you to meet with the policy aide when that person's in town. It is always best when you have direct contact with *both* the legislator and the policy person.

The officeholders themselves do hold regular district meetings and often enjoy coming out to see you if you have something interesting to show them. They are generally pretty good about that and like seeing your organization in action if you plan well in advance. Still, it's just not the same as being up close and personal at the state capitol where business gets done. It's also an amazingly cool experience to lobby at your state's capitol, in part because the capitol buildings themselves are incredibly interesting places to visit. Therefore, if the issue is something that you care about deeply, you've got to find a way to make the journey by plane, train, bus, or automobile. The investment of time and money will be well worth it, assuming you've done your homework first.

IT'S SHOW TIME!

So here you are. You've done your background work. You've set up and confirmed appointments in advance with as many legislative offices as possible prior to your visit. You've made copies of your fact sheet, position paper, and press coverage. You've rehearsed, and you've coordinated your schedules to know that you've set aside enough time in between appointments to get from one meeting to another (or have decided that, if need be, you'll split up the team if appointments run overtime). You've practiced your talking points, ironed your clothes (or at least made sure they aren't stained), pooled your pennies to get there, and then, finally, you've arrived! You've made it! It's huge! It's beautiful! It's scary! Now what?

You'll find your way to the legislator's office to begin your first meeting (or perhaps meet online). You and your team members will start the meeting by thanking the person, whether the elected official or that person's proxy, for meeting with you. Then you'll thank the Senator, Assembly Member, Representative, Delegate, Supervisor, Councilmember, or whoever it is you're lobbying for that person's long-standing support of XYZ issues. Why do you acknowledge the legislator's work in this area? Because it shows you are familiar with that person's work and the causes they hold dear. If this is a newly elected official who doesn't have a legislative track record, you might draw on what you learned from the research you did during the mapping stage. For instance, you might say, "As a proud soccer mom, we think you'll be able to relate to the need to mandate background checks for all people who coach school sport teams." Either of these strategies will pave the way for the legislator or that person's aide being receptive to what you have to say. And if all of this sounds familiar from what I already said about making the initial phone call, it is!

You'll then use your fact sheet to briefly present your case—pointing out the key facts related to the problem, your proposed solution, and the coalition of organizations that have signed on to your effort. Your fact sheet is the story board for your campaign and should guide the talking points for your presentation. If you are meeting in person, put it on the table between you and the person you're lobbying and point to each area you want to cover. That will help keep your messaging on track.

The person you're meeting with will probably ask you a number of questions about your issue. Just like Jeff McDonald of *The San Diego Union-Tribune* advised us about talking to the media in Chapter 10, be sure to tell the truth. If you don't know the answer to something, let that person know you're happy to find it out and will be back in touch once you do. You'll learn for the most part that whomever you're speaking to will give you undivided attention.

People will probably be gracious as well, even if they disagree with what you have to say. Those who are most interested in your issue will ask for a copy of your white paper so that they can read about it in greater detail. If the meeting seems to be going well and you're done answering all of their questions, *be sure to ask directly if the legislator would be willing to author a bill of this nature.* It's unlikely that you'll get an answer on the spot, but the response you do receive will give you an indication of how interested that office is in your issue.

Let's say, though, for the moment, that you meet with Representative McGinness and he *loves* your idea and understands immediately why it's important. It's just that, well, he's carrying too many other bills at the moment, and he thinks your idea needs to be modified somewhat in order to make it palatable to the other members of his committee (and, eventually, to the larger group of legislators). That scenario is more likely to happen than not. Often, you'll walk in with a *big* idea (although it may not seem so big at the time) and come out with a smaller version of that idea. It might not even happen at the first office. For instance, as much as Representative Ramirez was able to wax poetically about your idea, Representative Brown wasn't nearly as crazy about it and didn't think it would fly at the committee level without some modifications. Then Representative Rosenberg added her 10 cents, and before you knew it, your idea looked a lot different than what you thought when you first woke up that morning.

Listen to what everyone has to say, and think carefully about whether these compromises will work for you. Don't negotiate away those things that are vitally important to your cause, but do consider what's possible. You may have to start at a different point and build up to what you want over a series of years. You might be lobbying in a year when money is extremely tight and there isn't any political will to launch a new program. Or maybe there's enough money to begin with a pilot program in one county to test your idea before it becomes available throughout the state. Passing legislation requires negotiation, cooperation, conciliation, and patience. It's like the words to that old Rolling Stones song, "You can't always get what you want. But if you try sometimes, you just might find, you get what you need."[i]

CATCHING FLIES WITH HONEY

Problems arise when advocates go into an elected official's office *demanding* that something happen. Advocates sometimes think that if they arrive with a hoard of people, campaign signs, and TV cameras in tow, then they will be sure to "win" their case. Actually, the opposite may happen. The legislator might be so offended by your group's pressure tactics that the door is slammed shut on your point of view—and on the people you're trying to help. If you were on the other end of that, you might do the same; no one I know responds well to that kind of situation.

There is an old saying "It's easier to catch flies with honey," which means that it's easier to attract someone to your side when you're being nice. No matter how tempted you may be, do not, under any circumstances, raise your voice in an argumentative or whiny tone to the people you are lobbying. It won't get you anywhere.

It is critically important that you act respectfully to the elected and appointed officials who serve our communities for the simple reason that if you are disrespectful to one, others who may have views much more similar to yours will be reluctant to work with you because they'll have heard about your behavior and be turned off by it (word travels fast). You may feel in your heart of hearts that your issue is *the* most important issue of the day and become frustrated if your local official doesn't agree. Remember, though, that this person has probably met with many other individuals and groups who feel similarly about the issue *they've* brought for consideration. Don't stomp your feet, try not to cry, keep it together, and make every effort to act professionally at all times. That includes being careful not to bad mouth an elected official or their staff in any hallway in the building—you never know who is walking by, and those corridors echo!

Thankfully we live in a country where we are allowed to express our views freely. Sometimes your elected officials have opinions that are vastly different from your own. When that's the case, the best thing to do is to work as hard as you can to educate them about the situation as you see it using the solid research you've taken the time to put together. If you are able to develop a relationship with that person over time, you might be surprised at how your mutual respect might evolve into support for the things you care about down the road.

Even with all of your advanced planning, there will be times when you are lobbying at your state capitol and realize that you want to drop in on someone you hadn't made an appointment to go see. It might be because that friendly aide in Senator Yang's office said, "Did you guys set up an appointment to talk to Senator Ahmed? She's really hot on this topic." And somehow you hadn't known that—perhaps because she was just sworn into office a few weeks earlier and, as much as you tried, you couldn't get much background information on her and her interests. It's OK to drop in on people without an appointment. You may get lucky and even be able to meet with Senator Ahmed herself. Sometimes you'll run into people on the elevator who you didn't expect to see and lobby them. The moral of the story is to bring along plenty of extra information packets.

After every meeting, act like ambassadors for Emily Post and write thank-you notes to each of the legislators and aides who took time to meet with you. Equally important, make sure that if people have agreed to author your bill, you get back to them as soon as humanly possible with the information they need. Letters from your constituents to various members of the committee will also be welcomed. And don't forget to keep generating positive press for your idea. If you find a legislator to author your bill, be sure to coordinate your press strategy with that office.

HOW THEY DID IT

This is it. All the roads we took during this process led us to this point. It's the moment of truth. If this were baseball, we would be the starting pitcher having already gone eight strong innings. Now, we also needed to be the closer if we were going for the complete game!

We did our research on who we should approach, which resulted in the list of legislators we would target. Since most of the work to support our cause took place during a graduate course, we had a pre-set date for when the entire class would fly to Sacramento to lobby on a single day (we were based in San Diego). We were concerned about being able to schedule all of the meetings that we needed to have on that one date. Luckily, it all worked out fine.

As we began contacting various legislators, or rather their aides, we found that a phone call often worked best. It was much harder for someone to say no to us on the phone than via e-mail. This initial conversation with the legislator's aide was critical

---

because they had the ability to get us a meeting or to send us on our way. We had to be clear, concise, and most of all, polite. Even if we got a no with regard to a meeting, we thanked them for their time and treated them with the utmost respect. Not only is this just common courtesy, you never know who you might run into at the capitol or whose support you might need at a later date!

We ended up scheduling several meetings at the capitol and we were so excited for our trip. Our months of hard work were finally coming to a head and would hopefully pay off. While at the capitol, some of our meetings were with aides, some were with legislators, yet we soon learned that both were equally important.

When we arrived, we were prepared and organized. We were also anxious and worried that no one would want to talk with us. We had all of our paperwork ready to go for each meeting, and even went the extra mile by printing it all in full color. Luckily, we decided to bring extra copies, so we were ready for any spontaneous, last-minute meetings. We wanted everything to look as professional as possible, including ourselves. We had rehearsed our presentation, and also knew that we had to be prepared to answer questions that people might throw at us. Although we had practiced a few days earlier and assigned each team member specific points to highlight, all of our preparations couldn't eliminate the fear that we might get it wrong. But the process turned out to be much easier and less formal—and the offices smaller—than we expected. Elected officials and their staff were welcoming and genuinely interested in what we had to say.

While most of our meetings did not lead to immediate action, one did. All you need is one legislator to be fully on board

continued from previous page

with your cause in the beginning to help move it forward. We were feeling optimistic during our meeting with Senator Simitian's aide. He appeared interested in the issue and carefully reviewed all of the materials we provided. He asked lots of questions. We shared key points from our research and told him that we knew Senator Simitian had authored a similar bill seven years earlier, back when he was an assemblymember, that did not pass. We talked about how many young people and their parents might have been helped if the previous bill *had* passed. He encouraged us to talk with aides in other legislators' offices, and even introduced us to some of his colleagues who worked for other senators. That led us to several unscheduled meetings.

The day was a whirlwind. People wanted to hear from us, and with each new conversation, it became easier and easier to talk about our issue. Shortly after our day of meetings, we were thrilled to learn that Senator Joe Simitian had decided to author an updated version of the bill! We were ecstatic. This visit was an important step, and yet we still had a long way to go before our bill would finally pass.

REFERENCE

i. The Rolling Stones. (1969). You can't always get what you want. On *Let It Bleed* [Studio album]. London: Olympic Studios.

Chapter 12

Step 10: Monitor Progress on the Issue

Getting to the Finish Line

I must begin this chapter with a confession. Naming this last step Monitor Progress on the Issue was not my finest moment; that title does a lousy job capturing what's involved in Step 10. I can't change it, though, because I've written other books and academic papers that have referenced the 10 Steps by name, so I'm stuck with it. If I got to rename it, I'd probably call it something like Getting to the Finish Line. In any event, this chapter walks you through what to do after a legislator agrees to author your bill, which, again, will probably be called something like an ordinance, measure, or resolution if it's happening locally. People think this part of the process is much more complicated than it really is! Trust me, once you've arrived here, you've already done most of the heavy lifting.

The road trip a bill makes as it travels from the time it is introduced to when it becomes law is fundamentally the same regardless of whether you're trying to pass something at the state or local level. It's kind of like reaching your destination traveling by highway, side streets, or country roads. That said, just as some state legislatures work full time and others part time, there are also differences in how local governments make laws depending on what type of government entity you're lobbying and where you live. To be sure you get it right, visit the state/county/city/town's website, choose an issue that got passed, and follow the process to see how it traveled. As my friend Steve Russell[1] says, "You'll want to backtrack to go forward." In a small city or town, for instance, there might be only one aide or one office that handles everything for all its legislators. That said, if you hop in my van, I'll give you a ride that I think will be pretty close to the one you'll take with your campaign pals.

HOW IT'S DONE

You've gotten to yes by finding an author[2] for your bill! After you jump up and down and high-five your group, what happens? The legislative aide will take the sample language you've provided, and that aide will be responsible for seeing that the bill language is created for your issue. The description of what you want to become law will be sent to an in-house attorney (that is, someone who works for that government entity) who will do the write up.

BUT even though these bill writers are professionals, you *still* need to read over what they've written to make sure that it matches your intent because mistakes happen, things can be misinterpreted, and ideas can get lost in translation. Remember, too, that whoever writes the bill works for the *legislator*—not *your* group—and will most often interact with the legislator's office to get an understanding of what needs to be written up. For this reason, you need to

---

1. One of the smartest people I've ever met, Steve is an advocate for affordable housing in San Diego.
2. A city or town may not use the term *author*, but the concept is the same.

develop a very close working relationship with the legislator's aide to make sure that your ideas don't get bungled like a bad game of telephone. Once the bill language is settled, a state bill will be introduced and assigned a number, which will make it easy to track; a local bill will get its number later on.

Since you've been following the bouncing ball throughout the 10 Steps, you know that the first place your bill will land for consideration is a committee hearing. The aide for the legislator who is carrying your bill will let you know when the hearing is scheduled and will talk you through what you can expect. In fact, that aide will act as your guide dog throughout this process—leading you through the pathways of the winding Yellow Brick Road I described in Chapter 1 until, hopefully, your bill becomes a law.

If you haven't already met all the members of the committee where your bill will be heard, now is the time to set up individual meetings with them so that you can make the rounds with your fact sheet and white paper. The purpose of these meetings is to ask these legislators to support bill #, the XYZ bill, which is being authored by legislator X. If you've already met with them once, touch base with them again, both to let them know that you've found a bill author and to formally ask for their support.

If you're lobbying at a county, city, or other local level, you'll need to make the rounds to meet with all the members of that entire body for the same purpose; for example, you'd meet with everyone who sits on the city council. When you do, be sure to have members of your coalition who vote in the districts of those legislators attend these meetings.

Regardless of whether you're operating at the state or local level, during your meetings with these elected officials you'll learn if they like your bill and plan to vote for it, are waffling on the issue, or object to your bill:

- If they plan to vote for your bill, be sure to send them a thank-you note from your coalition acknowledging how much you appreciate their support. If their staff person was helpful, be sure to mention that person by name. Mailed notes are *always* preferable to e-mails, although e-mails will do in a pinch if the timetable between your meeting and the bill hearing is tight. I know this might seem old fashioned, but it is in keeping with the dignity of the officeholder. Personalized thank-you calls, notes, and e-mails from people who live in and are registered to vote in their district will be appreciated as well. In other words, people shouldn't act like Broadway stars by reading or writing their comments from a script.
- If elected officials are waffling on the issue, be sure to generate personalized e-mails, notes (time permitting), and phone calls in support of the bill from folks who belong to your coalition, live in their district, and are registered to vote as it is likely that the person answering the phone will ask for the caller's address.

You'd be surprised by how much these communications make a difference—especially if they are heartfelt—because not nearly enough people communicate with their elected officials on issues. As a result, when legislators hear from several constituents on a single issue, it can really make a *big* difference; the more that come in, the more influence they have on whether a bill will pass through committee.

The folks from your coalition who met with the legislator should also send a thank-you note. The note should thank them for their time and consideration, repeat your main talking points about why the bill is important, and let them know again how to contact you if they have further questions.

- If they're negative about the issue, do your best to listen patiently to their objections without getting angry. I know, this is easier said than done. If you think they have raised a legitimate concern that you hadn't considered, address it with the legislator who is authoring the bill. Later on, your bill's author can amend the bill to add this provision, and if your negative nelly knows that upfront, that might change his vote to a yes.

And, finally (as if you didn't already know!): Write that person a thank-you note—thanking them for their time, recapping your request, and letting them know how to contact you with questions. Also generate calls, e-mails, letters, and postcards, (time permitting), from people who live in and are registered to vote in that person's district.

To state the obvious, all of this requires a lot of coordination and coaching on good communication strategies. The bottom line is that you can never say thank you enough times.

DO I HEAR AN "AMEN?!" TESTIFYING

When your bill comes up for a hearing, you'll have an opportunity to testify. The aide to the legislator who is authoring your bill will give you the lowdown on what to expect—how long you should speak, how many people from your coalition can talk, and tips for how to shape your testimony based on what that aide has been hearing from the other members and their staff. Even though your group will have met with all or most of those members, it's always helpful to have an insider's perspective. Those insights will help you formulate a strategy for your testimony.

Testifying is not as scary as it sounds because you'll be incredibly well-prepared by this point and are also allowed to use notes and charts. The simple trick that I've learned over the years is to rehearse an endless number of times until I'm sick of listening to my own voice and have pretty much memorized what I plan to say. On the day of the hearing, you'll want to bring along as many members of your coalition as possible. Even though only a few will be able to testify, others can fill the room with signs or T-shirts that show they are affiliated with your campaign. The most valuable speakers will be people who have been directly affected by the issue because their remarks will be the most compelling. If you are able to generate additional press coverage for your issue right before the hearing, that will also be extremely helpful because it will show the lawmakers that the public is paying attention to your issue.

After the bill passes through the committee, the first thing you should do is thank the members of the committee who voted for it as well as the legislator who authored the bill and the staff person who assisted you. Depending on the issue you're working on, it may be referred to another committee, like a fiscal committee if the bill has a high cost, or another issue committee (for instance, a Housing, Environment, or Transportation Committee) might hear the same bill.

If your campaign involves a local issue, your work is almost done. The next step will be for your issue to be heard before the full body. Obviously, you'll need to meet with all of those folks if you haven't already. Once that body meets and passes your bill, you're nearly done. Remember, the chief elected official, like a mayor, *may* have the option of vetoing the measure depending on what kind of legislative body it is and, if you're at the city level, whether or not you have a strong mayor form of government. If you do have a chief executive with veto power, be sure to lobby that person while your ordinance is working its way through the council. Remember, though, that vetoes can be overturned by a majority or supermajority vote depending on the charter for your local government.

NEXT UP AT THE STATE LEVEL: A FLOOR VOTE

If you're working on a state bill, the next stage in its life will be a vote on the floor of the same legislative chamber. In other words, if your bill started in the Senate or House, all members of the Senate or House will now have the opportunity to vote on it. An exception would be if the bill has to be heard in a fiscal committee, such as Appropriations, because it carries a high price tag or has a companion issue committee like the ones I mentioned earlier. If that's the case, you'd repeat all of the things I already talked about—testifying, meeting with committee members, generating calls and letters, etc.—before it would (hopefully) move to a floor vote.

When it's scheduled for a floor vote, you'll want to be sure to touch base with your bill's author, or their staff person, to get a read on who else your coalition may need to contact with calls and letters in support of your bill. In other words, there will be legislators who are not on the committee who may have questions about it. You'll want to rally people from their districts who know your talking points to reach out to those legislators.

Once a bill passes the house of origin, you'll need to thank the bill's author again. (Yes, this is a lot of thank-you's; however, you can never make a mistake by building too much goodwill!) Next, you'll regroup to testify and appear at a committee hearing on the bill in the *other* chamber, so if it started on the House side, you'll have a do-over on the Senate side, or vice versa. At this point, you'll be old pros, so it should go smoothly! Just like last time, you'll want members of your coalition to reach out to the legislators who are on that committee prior to the hearing with e-mails and phone calls of support. Ideally, the bill will pass through the committee, after which members of your coalition should generate thank-you e-mails and phone calls to the committee members. Then, just as it did in the first house, it will go to the floor of the second house for a full vote.

By the time your bill passes both houses, you'll be so close to home that you'll almost be able to smell whatever your family has bubbling on the stove. Still, your bill won't become a law until the governor signs it. Once that happens, you can jump up and down, scream for joy, and do a celebratory dance (at least, that's what I do).

WHAT IF IT DOESN'T GO AS PLANNED?

Way back in the first chapter of the book, I mentioned two things that could go wrong. One is that the governor could veto your bill. If that happens, you'll need to muster up a supermajority of votes in each house to override that veto in order for your bill to become a law. While that's not an easy thing to do, it's not impossible. Probably the best thing to do in that instance is to try again during the next legislative session, while incorporating a strategy to educate the governor's office, generate more press, and get more calls and correspondence from folks in your coalition and people of influence to weigh in on the issue.

The other thing I want to remind you is that a bill must pass each chamber with the *exact same language* in order to be on its way to becoming a law. Sometimes there are bumps along this road. Your bill might pass the second house with different language than when it passed in the house where it started. In that instance, your bill will need to go back to its house of origin for a *concurrence vote*—that is, an up-or-down vote on the language put in by the second house. If the bill fails, or the house of origin does not "concur," your bill is not necessarily dead. It could still be referred to a conference commit-tee, where there will be some give and take of ideas from each house. If an agreement is reached there, then the conference committee issues a revised version of the bill that will go to each house for an up-or-down vote. However, if your bill fails on concurrence very late in the legislative session, there may not be time for a conference committee.

It can be heartbreaking when a bill passes one house but not another, like background checks for gun purchases; however, your experience during that first go-round will hopefully give you the information you need to reformulate a strategy for the following legislative session. What you learned during the mapping and lob-bying process—particularly regarding the web of friendships and relationships—should help you bridge differences across the aisle. There may also be newly elected legislators who enter the picture and put the odds in your favor next time. Don't despair: Even though Annamarie and Travis had great luck and an awesome strategy for getting their bill passed in a single legislative session, it sometimes takes years for good legislation to pass.

If you have the skill and good fortune to have your bill pass, you'll want to be sure to publicly thank the legislators who worked with you. You can recognize their leadership by inviting them to speak at a gathering of your coalition, posting a photo of them on your website, or mentioning them in a news story on the bill's pas-sage (be sure to coordinate your press strategy with the legislator's office). Passing legislation is about good preparedness, and it's also about maintaining good relationships. Besides, you never know when you might decide to use the 10 Steps to pass another law!

HOW THEY DID IT

With our meetings in Sacramento behind us, we were now looking forward to hearing about how our bill was progressing from its author, Senator Simitian. Of course, we say "our" bill, but in actuality, we didn't get any sort of recognition. A local Sheriff's office was instead mentioned as the group that helped bring this bill to prominence because they were the ones who had proposed it years earlier. It didn't matter to us. What mattered was getting our bill passed because of the positive impact it was going to have on young people in our state. That's what we cared about. At the same time, it was very satisfying to see that some of the research and language from the white paper and fact sheet we had prepared was included in memos from Senator Simitian's office when he began the process of engaging other legislators to support the bill.

Although our class had ended with the trip to Sacramento in January, the legislative process follows an entirely different timeline. Our group continued to meet, make phone calls, and send e-mails to help engage more supporters until the bill finally passed in May. The legislative aide we first met during our visit to the capitol became our regular contact for updates, encouraged us to keep requesting letters of support, and invited us to come to Sacramento again once the hearings were underway. He kept us informed when the bill moved from each committee and was finally ready to move to the Assembly and Senate. He even asked us to select our preferred date when scheduling the Senate hearing to make sure that Annamarie could testify about her son's experiences with DXM.

continued from previous page

Sadly, though, Annamarie wasn't able to travel to Sacramento to testify because her son was hospitalized for addiction shortly before the final hearings. It was the height of irony. She was prepared and looking forward to telling her family's story with the hope that her first-hand account might influence legislators to vote in the bill's favor. Although it would not be possible for her to be there in person, the fact that so many people were determined to pass this bill made this personally difficult period a little easier for Annamarie to bear. Senator Simitian's aide continued to share reports from the hearings. We soon learned that the bill passed 37-0! The Assembly followed suit with a similar home run.

While we were prepared for the worst, we always hoped for the best. In terms of getting updates from Senator Simitian's office, we found that it was up to our group to find out how things were progressing. Keeping in close contact with our legislator's aide worked out well; he was always willing to share any updates he had. In addition, instead of simply asking him how things were going, we went a step further by continually asking how we and our coalition could be of assistance. Showing our willingness to stay involved helped us stay in the know!

After several months and a few different iterations, our bill successfully made it through the House and Senate. All that was left for our months of hard work, our countless hours, and our trials and tribulations to finally pay off was a little, itty-bitty, teeny-tiny signature. And it happened. Governor Jerry Brown signed our bill, SB 514, into law on August 31, 2011. We had done it!

We came into this journey with no experience in lobbying and an idea of a change we thought would benefit young people. Step by step, everything came together. While it wasn't easy, it also wasn't the hardest thing to do, either. Anyone, and we mean *anyone*, can do this. While things may seem daunting initially, just remember to take it one step at a time. YOU CAN DO THIS!

When we started out, we had no idea that we would ever be successful in having legislation passed. Ultimately, we all felt empowered by the fact that everything we did along the way worked. Our efforts made it a little bit easier for other families to protect their children and keep them safer.

Now What? It Ain't Over
When It's Over

There's nothing like that giddy feeling once you've passed a law. And I think that feeling is 10 times stronger when you've done it using a combination of good research, people power, and common sense without having to spend more than a few dollars on paper and gas. So, before you worry about what's next, be sure to take some time to celebrate.

After your law has passed, your campaign may seem like it's over, but it really isn't. Your coalition will still have to spend time making sure that what passed is put into effect in the way you intended. Sadly, you may have to monitor this for years to come. If you look at how the 1965 Voting Rights Act unraveled in recent years, you'll know what I mean.[1]

There are three key things that you'll need to pay attention to that I'll touch upon briefly:

1. **Regulations.** Hopefully, you put some thought into how you imagined your idea would work on the ground. It's hugely important that you take some time to meet with the people who will be responsible for carrying out the law, both to

---

1. "As of May, 2021, 17 states enacted 28 new laws that restrict access to the vote." *Source:* https://www.brennancenter.org/our-work/research-reports/voting-laws-roundup -may-2021 This is in response to the 2013 Supreme Court Ruling that gut major provisions in the voting rights act.

make sure that your vision matches theirs and to offer any insights you gained through your research. It will be helpful if the legislator, or at least, the legislative aide you worked with, accompanies you to the initial meeting with these administrators. That will signal the legislator is keeping tabs on what the administrators are doing, which is important because the legislature has the power to make sure the bill is being carried out according to its intended purpose.

To emphasize a point that I've made throughout this book, be sure this meeting includes representatives from your group who either have lived experience with this issue or will be directly affected by the law that is carried out. And just as you prepared carefully for your initial meetings with legislators, be sure to prepare for this meeting as well. Try to find out whether or not the administrators are going to be excited about or resistant to implementing the law. Fortunately, you developed a lot of skills and strategies during the process of passing a law that you can make use of in this stage of the process (particularly Step 6, Brand the Issue, and Step 9, Approach Elected Officials).

2. **Funding.** Sometimes your bill will pass but there won't be money in the budget to carry out whatever is in it. If you need money, honey, you should try to make sure that funding for it has been allocated in the budget of the entity you've been lobbying. Alternatively, you and the legislative aide can meet with officials at the agency that will carry out the work to ensure that money can be found for that purpose. You'll of course want to refer back to the research you did in Step 2 to determine the cost of implementing your idea.

3. **Repeal.** Just because you won the battle to pass your bill, that doesn't mean the other side has stopped fighting. Keep your eyes and ears open to any new legislation that is designed to unravel your ball of yarn. If things are heating up, you'll want to put together a group who will take responsibility for continually updating your list of supporters and detractors (Step 5).

Throughout these activities, remember to continue practicing the skills you learned throughout the lobbying process—bring along helpful information, thank the people who are working with you, and maintain positive working relationships. If things don't go as well as planned, you can always activate your coalition for help and support.

As for the DXM campaign, the whole thing worked like a charm. Whenever I buy cough medicine at the Rite Aid, the clerk asks me for my ID. It's that simple. Who knows how many kids have been stopped from spiraling into substance abuse because Annamarie, Travis, and a few friends took the time to make sure this law exists? They didn't even follow the 10 Steps perfectly, and their campaign still worked!

If you've learned anything from reading these chapters, I hope it's this: You don't have to be a corporate bigwig or loud-mouth powerbroker to lobby legislators. Normal, everyday citizens like you can create meaningful change for yourself and others in your community by using the 10 Steps, or your own version of them (maybe you do hip-hop instead of a line dance or a polka?). Regardless of how you do it, it's up to each of us to take a stand for what we believe is important. It's empowering to go through the process. It's incredibly rewarding when we succeed.

At the beginning, just thinking about trying to create or change a law can feel overwhelming. We know the stakes are high, which sometimes leads us to believe that we should leave the heavy lifting to others: people who in our minds are more experienced, or probably better at this than we are. To respond to those thoughts and doubts, I'll leave you with a quote from the ancient sage Hillel: "If I am not for myself, who will be for me? If I am not for others, what am I? And if not now, when?"

APPENDIX

Legal Lobbying Rules for Nonprofits

I'm going to begin with an amazing but little-known fact: It is 100% legal for nonprofit 501(c)(3) corporations[1] to lobby! Sadly, the vast majority of people who are connected to these nonprofits don't know this or don't understand the law and, as a result, don't lobby. It breaks my heart, which is why I've written this appendix specifically for folks who work for or volunteer with 501(c)(3)s.[2] In fact, studies show that when nonprofit staff understand the law and have the support of their board, they're more likely to lobby.[i] That's why I'm passionate about explaining the rules and regulations here in a way that will be easy for everyone to understand.

---

1. 501(c)(3) private foundations have much greater limits on lobbying than 501(c)(3) charities, although they can provide grants that can be used for lobbying!
2. There are actually 27 different IRS classifications of nonprofit corporation types! This chapter is focusing ONLY on 501(c)(3)s, which are the most common type of nonprofit.

THERE ARE TWO CHOICES

Since nonprofit activities are governed by tax law, the IRS oversees and enforces nonprofit lobbying regulations. And as weird as this may seem, the most current nonprofit lobbying laws they're working from were passed by Congress way back in 1976![3]

When it comes to regulations, complexity is the enemy of good. Unfortunately, that's true in this case, where there are two *different* sets of rules that nonprofits can use to lobby and account for their lobbying activities. I'll explain them here.

First, from the minute they receive their incorporation papers, nonprofits are born with the right to lobby to a limited extent under something called the *substantial part test*. At its most basic, this means that lobbying can't be a substantial part of a nonprofit's activities (measured by the things it does as well as by the money, staff, and volunteer time spent to do them). I can't tell you, though, what *substantial* means under these rules because, well, no one has ever defined it. So, if your nonprofit is lobbying under the substantial part test, you're more or less winging it.

Alternatively, nonprofits that aren't specifically formed for religious purposes, like a church, mosque, synagogue, Buddhist temple, etc.,[4] can choose to come under something called the *expenditure test*, otherwise known as the *501(h) election*. I always say the "h" stands for "have at it, have fun, go lobby!" because choosing the expenditure test is as easy as pie and opens up a clearly defined set of rules that allows a nonprofit lots of room to lobby. As an added bonus, if you or your board are worry warts, there is actually *less* need to fret about stepping on anyone's toes at the IRS because the guidelines are straightforward, generous in terms of what you can do, and make recordkeeping even easier than if you

3. Although the regs for these laws weren't released until 1990!
4. There are a few other 501(c)(3) types that are also prohibited from choosing the (h)—like Legal Aid Societies, for example—but the vast majority are free to enjoy the gifts of 501 (h).

lobby under the substantial part test. (And no, the IRS is *not* more likely to audit your organization if you choose the 501(h) election)!

So, how does it work? To start the ball rolling, a nonprofit files a teeny, tiny form—Form 5768, which takes, at most, three minutes to fill out—with the IRS to elect to measure its lobbying activities under the expenditure test (see next page).

After an organization signs up, its status is automatically granted, is retroactive to the beginning of the fiscal year for that nonprofit, and never has to be renewed! That retroactive part is especially wonderful in case your organization has been coloring way outside the lines with its lobbying activities and was starting to get sweaty palms about possibly violating the law. Once you file the 501(h) election, your organization will report its annual lobbying expenses (if it has any) on its Form 990 (the annual tax return).

THE MAGIC OF THE 501(h) ELECTION

The expenditure test can be summed up in one way—an organization is lobbying *only* when it spends money on activities that are explicitly defined as lobbying. Those are:

- When it states its position on specific legislation to legislators (and/or their staff)—this is *direct lobbying*.
- When it communicates its position on specific legislation to the general public and issues a "call to action" that asks them to contact their legislators about supporting that position—this is *grassroots lobbying*.

If your nonprofit doesn't spend money on these things, it's not lobbying. Period. It's important to remember, though, that if your staff does this kind of work, their time counts as an expense because they don't work for free.

Form **5768**

(Rev. September 2016)

Department of the Treasury
Internal Revenue Service

**Election/Revocation of Election by an Eligible
Section 501(c)(3) Organization To Make
Expenditures To Influence Legislation**
(Under Section 501(h) of the Internal Revenue Code)
▶ Information about Form 5768 and its instructions is at *www.irs.gov/form5768.*

For IRS
Use Only ▶

Name of organization	Employer identification number

Number and street (or P.O. box no., if mail is not delivered to street address)	Room/suite

City, town or post office, and state	ZIP + 4

1 Election— As an eligible organization, we hereby elect to have the provisions of section 501(h) of the Code, relating to expenditures to influence legislation, apply to our tax year ending _____ and all subsequent tax years until revoked. *(Month, day, and year)*

Note: This election must be signed and postmarked within the first taxable year to which it applies.

2 Revocation— As an eligible organization, we hereby revoke our election to have the provisions of section 501(h) of the Code, relating to expenditures to influence legislation, apply to our tax year ending _____ and all subsequent tax years *(until a new election is made).* *(Month, day, and year)*

Note: This revocation must be signed and postmarked before the first day of the tax year to which it applies.

Under penalties of perjury, I declare that I am authorized to make this (check applicable box) ▶ ☐ election ☐ revocation
on behalf of the above named organization.

_____
(Signature of officer or trustee)

_____
(Type or print name and title)

_____
(Date)

General Instructions

*Section references are to the Internal
Revenue Code.*

Section 501(c)(3) states that an organization exempt under that section will lose its tax-exempt status and its qualification to receive deductible charitable contributions if a substantial part of its activities are carried on to influence legislation. Section 501(h), however, permits certain eligible section 501(c)(3) organizations to elect to make limited expenditures to influence legislation. An organization making the election will, however, be subject to an excise tax under section 4911 if it spends more than the amounts permitted by that section. Also, the organization may lose its exempt status if its lobbying expenditures exceed the permitted amounts by more than 50% over a 4-year period. For any tax year in which an election under section 501(h) is in effect, an electing organization must report the actual and permitted amounts of its lobbying expenditures and grass roots expenditures (as defined in section 4911(c)) on its annual return required under section 6033. See Part II-A of Schedule C (Form 990 or Form 990-EZ). Each electing member of an affiliated group must report these amounts for both itself and the affiliated group as a whole.

To make or revoke the election, enter the ending date of the tax year to which

the election or revocation applies in item 1 or 2, as applicable, and sign and date the form in the spaces provided.

Eligible organizations. A section 501(c)(3) organization is permitted to make the election if it is not a disqualified organization (see below) and is described in:

1. Section 170(b)(1)(A)(ii) (relating to educational institutions),
2. Section 170(b)(1)(A)(iii) (relating to hospitals and medical research organizations),
3. Section 170(b)(1)(A)(iv) (relating to organizations supporting government schools),
4. Section 170(b)(1)(A)(vi) (relating to organizations publicly supported by charitable contributions),
5. Section 170(b)(1)(A)(ix) (relating to agricultural research organizations),
6. Section 509(a)(2) (relating to organizations publicly supported by admissions, sales, etc.), or
7. Section 509(a)(3) (relating to organizations supporting certain types of public charities other than those section 509(a)(3) organizations that support section 501(c)(4), (5), or (6) organizations).

Disqualified organizations. The following types of organizations are not permitted to make the election:

a. Section 170(b)(1)(A)(i) organizations (relating to churches),

b. An integrated auxiliary of a church or of a convention or association of churches, or

c. A member of an affiliated group of organizations if one or more members of such group is described in **a** or **b** of this paragraph.

Affiliated organizations. Organizations are members of an affiliated group of organizations only if (1) the governing instrument of one such organization requires it to be bound by the decisions of the other organization on legislative issues, or (2) the governing board of one such organization includes persons (i) who are specifically designated representatives of another such organization or are members of the governing board, officers, or paid executive staff members of such other organization, and (ii) who, by aggregating their votes, have sufficient voting power to cause or prevent action on legislative issues by the first such organization.

For more details, see section 4911 and section 501(h).

Note: A private foundation (including a private operating foundation) is not an eligible organization.

Where to file. Mail Form 5768 to:

Department of the Treasury
Internal Revenue Service Center
Ogden, UT 84201-0027

Cat. No. 12125M

Form **5768** (Rev. 9-2016)

Let's dig a bit deeper into those terms—*direct lobbying, grassroots lobbying,* and *call to action.*

Direct Lobbying

Direct lobbying is pretty much what it sounds like. It happens when you or *anyone* from your nonprofit contacts an elected official (or their wonderful aide) with a direct request to act (pro or con) on a specific piece of legislation at the federal, state, or local level. This includes asking for money for your nonprofit's operations, for the work you do, for your community, or for the people you serve because budgets are also legislation. So, if you're trying to persuade members of your city council to increase funding for parks and recreation, that funding will be part of the city budget and is, therefore, considered legislation.

You're also directly lobbying when you ask the public to vote a certain way on a ballot question since the outcome of that vote will determine whether or not that law passes. Let's say, for example, that your nonprofit is trying to pass a ballot measure[5] to raise taxes for affordable housing, and it encourages people to vote yes by spreading the word through free and paid media/social media advertising. That's direct lobbying, which makes your expenses for that campaign direct lobbying expenses. You can think of it his way: If you're contacting the decider,[6] you're engaging in direct lobbying.

---

5. There are all kinds of things a nonprofit can legally do to support or oppose a ballot measure. Your organization can have volunteers or staff gather signatures; loan or give money to ballot campaigns; buy TV, radio, Internet, or newspaper ads; or make statements in support of or opposition to a state or local ballot measure. Be careful, though! Even though this is all OK with the IRS, state campaign finance laws may have reporting, disclaimer, or other requirements. Check the law in your state before launching your effort to support or oppose a ballot measure, and also visit bolderadvocacy.org for insider tips.

6. And as you know from reading the previous chapters, that includes a legislator's staff.

Grassroots Lobbying

Grassroots lobbying happens when you ask the general public—or a portion of them (this doesn't include people who are members of your nonprofit)—to contact their elected officials about taking action on a specific piece of legislation that those legislators are considering. If you said, "Please call your city councilmember about allocating an additional 15% in the budget for afterschool programs at public libraries," that's grassroots lobbying because the councilmembers, not individual citizens, will ultimately decide whether there's more money for libraries in the annual city budget.

CALL TO ACTION

The term *call to action* is tied to grassroots lobbying. That's when your nonprofit urges citizens in your community to take action on a specific piece of legislation. Those instructions might be, "Call, write, sign a petition, and/or make an appointment to speak to your state senator about SB 123 and why it's important that everyone in your state has access to clean drinking water." Or a call to action could be more subtle, such as providing an online form that people can use to send a message to their lawmakers, or even simply giving them the contact information for their legislators. The key to something being a call to action is that you are telling folks to take direct action on a specific piece of legislation. When those annoying people ring my doorbell at dinner time to ask for money to help the environment, they are not issuing a call to action; they are simply being annoying. It only becomes a call to action if they ask me to sign a petition, make a call, send an email, etc.

If your nonprofit is operating under the 501(h) election/expenditure test, the amount it can spend on lobbying depends on its *exempt purpose expenditures*. Exempt purpose expenditures are basically what it costs your nonprofit to accomplish its mission (although it doesn't include amounts paid for fundraising operations or consultants). You can find this info on your Form 990.

Lobbying Ceilings Under the 1976 Lobby Law

Annual Exempt-Purpose Expenditures	Total Direct Lobbying Expenditures Allowable	Total Grassroots Lobbying Expenditures Allowable
Up to $500,000	20% of exempt-purpose expenditures up to $100,000	One-quarter of the total direct lobbying expenditure ceiling
$500,000–$1 million	$100,000 + 15% of excess over $500,000	$25,000 + 3.75% of excess over $500,000
$1 million–$1.5 million	$175,000 + 10% of excess over $1 million	$43,750 + 2.5% of excess over $1 million
$1.5 million–$17 million	$225,000 + 5% of excess over $1.5 million	$56,250 + 1.25% of excess over $1.5 million
Over $17 million	$1 million	$250,000

This chart shows you what your nonprofit can spend on lobbying (remember, even though this chart is dated 1976, this is still the current law). As you can see, it operates on a sliding scale—what you can spend depends on your annual expenditures.[7]

The big takeaway is that a nonprofit can spend a TON of dough relative to its overall operating costs on lobbying! Check it out—if your group is focused on a ballot campaign, that's *direct lobbying*, so you can legally spend 100% of your allocation on that campaign! What you can't do is spend more than 25% of your overall lobbying limit on grassroots lobbying (which can be a

7. For big organizations (those with annual exempt purpose expenditures of $17 million or more), there is a cap on lobbying of $1 million per year. Hopefully having this much money is a "problem" that your organization has or will have to worry about someday!

drag if you're committed to getting the public energized to work on your issue).

One other HUGE bonus of the 501(h) election is that a nonprofit can spend more than it's legally allowed to on lobbying in a single year and still be within the law because the IRS allows organizations to average out these activities and expenses over a four-year period. You'd have to exceed 150% of your limits during that time to lose your tax-exempt status! In contrast, a nonprofit that doesn't choose the 501(h) could, in theory, lose its tax-exempt status for doing "substantial" lobbying in a single year!

MORE BENEFITS OF 501(h)!

If your nonprofit chooses to come under the expenditure test, the IRS gives you LOTS of leeway on what you can do AND allows you to do these things without having to keep track of the time and money you spend doing them![8] To be clear, if you *don't* file the 501(h) election, your nonprofit will have to track all of these activities (regardless of whether they're done by staff or volunteers) and report them on your Form 990.

Here's what's allowable:

- Influencing regulations.
- Certain member communications.
- Invited testimony (or other technical assistance).
- Discussion of broad social and economic issues.
- Nonpartisan research and analysis.
- "Self-defense" lobbying.

8. Your nonprofit should always check state and local lobbying disclosure laws. These laws won't limit how much lobbying you can do, but they might require your nonprofit to register and report on some of these activities as "lobbying" (even if the IRS doesn't require it).

Let's unpack what each of these things means under the law.

Influencing Regulations

Once you succeed in creating a law, it'll probably go through a process to flesh out how it will be implemented. Under the 501(h) election, any time and money you spend to influence regulations doesn't need to be tracked and reported.

Certain Member Communications

The IRS defines a member of your organization as someone who contributes money to you as a member or volunteers for your nonprofit. Your nonprofit doesn't need to track the time and money you spend communicating with your members about legislation, even if you take a position on it, as long as you don't directly ask them to lobby. This is similar to grassroots lobbying in that there has to be a call to action in order for these activities to count as lobbying. So, if you send out an email or post on your website "We're working hard to get the city to make Fiesta Island a leash-free dog park and have been meeting regularly with members of the mayor's office and city council to lobby them on this issue," that doesn't count as lobbying because you're simply providing an update—you haven't asked your members to do anything.

It *does* count as lobbying when you ask your members to contact their lawmakers about a legislative proposal, but you get to treat that communication as direct lobbying rather than grassroots lobbying, which is great because as you know from reading the chart, the limits on direct lobbying are bigger. The only time a communication to your members is considered grassroots lobbying is when you ask them to help get other people in the community to contact their elected officials about the issue.

Invited Testimony (and Other Technical Assistance)

A major theme of the 10 Steps involves you or other members of your coalition becoming so knowledgeable about your issue that you've turned into a walking Wikipedia page. You know, too, that testifying before a committee about your issue is a major part of lobbying for it. If the committee that is hearing the bill asks you or your organization *in writing* to testify, then all the time you spend preparing to testify and delivering the testimony does not count as lobbying. This is referred to as the *technical advice exception*. The same is true if you give advice to a committee (for instance, helping them draft the bill).

Discussion of Broad Social and Economic Issues

If your organization is working on a bill about, say, health care reform and you hold a conference about health care reform, the activities related to hosting that event don't count as lobbying as long as you don't push specific legislation during a speech or conference workshop. To state the obvious, the same is true if you're working on any other topic.

Nonpartisan Research and Analysis

You *don't* have to count anything related to the gazillion hours you spend doing research, analysis, and writing your white paper as long as that work is nonpartisan. This is true even if your nonprofit takes a position on legislation and sends it to legislators. Research is considered nonpartisan if it gives a full and fair explanation of the facts and allows a reader to form an independent opinion. You also need to be able to show that there was a primary nonlobbying purpose for doing the work in the first place. You do this by showing that you distributed the materials to the same extent for nonlobbying purposes before or at the same time that you used them for lobbying. One thing to be careful of: If you take a position on legislation *and* issue a call to action, then it won't fall within this exception—it will count as *grassroots lobbying*.

"Self-Defense" Lobbying

The "self-defense" provision is a little tricky. It only applies to issues that directly affect your rights, tax-exempt status, or existence as a nonprofit entity—for example, if you lobby to protect property tax exemptions for nonprofits in your state or for legislation that would give nonprofit staff special tax advantages. In other words, the rule applies to both "offense" and "defense."

What surprisingly does *not* qualify for the self-defense exception is lobbying to protect your nonprofit from budget cuts or lobbying on causes that are at heart of your mission, such as an environmental organization opposing legislation that would weaken clean air laws.

A last word about these regs is a simple reminder that regardless of whether you choose the 501(h) election or decide to live in the uncertain world of whatever *substantial* means, you'll have to figure out a simple way to track your lobbying costs so that you can report them on your Form 990. This isn't difficult, and there are lots of online resources available to help you.

SHOW ME THE MONEY: FUNDING YOUR CAMPAIGN

There is only one source of money that you can *never* use to fund your lobbying work, and that is any type of government money.

Because of that, many nonprofits WRONGLY believe that if they receive any government money, they can't lobby at all. This makes me really mad, which is why I wrote the word *wrongly* in all caps.

There are many other sources of lobbying funds, including:

- **Individual contributions!** The most flexible funding source is money from membership dues, donations, and special events.
- **Community foundations!** Community foundations and donor-advised funds can earmark grants for lobbying and can even lobby themselves! This is because community foundations are public charities under the law (since they receive their funding from more than just one or a few sources).
- **Private foundations!** Although private foundations are kissing cousins to charitable 501(c)(3) nonprofits, they themselves can only lobby in very limited circumstances. BUT, they can provide operating grants to nonprofits that can be used for lobbying (as long as there's nothing in writing indicating that the foundation knows the funds will be used or "earmarked" for this purpose). They can also fund a project that involves lobbying if the project budget shows that multiple funders are underwriting that work and the nonlobbying part of budget is larger than the amount the foundation is providing.

FOR OVERACHIEVERS WHO EMBRACE THE DREAM

If your nonprofit becomes super involved in lobbying as a result of reading this book, two things will happen: 1) my wildest dreams will have come true, and 2) you may need to register as a lobbyist with your city or state. Each government entity has its own regulations—just be sure to find out what they are. The National Council of Nonprofits (http://www.councilofnonprofits.org/) will have state-level info. There are, of course, requirements for federal lobbying that you can find by looking up the Lobbying Disclosure Act of 1995.

You might also decide that your nonprofit wants to spend even more time lobbying than is allowable under the 501(h) election. If so, you could consider forming a sister (or brother) corporation, such as a 501(c)(4) nonprofit that can lobby with *no* limitations and can also endorse or oppose candidates for public office (although this can only be a secondary activity). The benefit of lobbying with no limitation comes with a trade-off; contributions to 501(c)(4) nonprofits are *not* tax deductible. Many well-known organizations, like Planned Parenthood Action Fund, the AARP, and the Sierra Club, have two sides to their work—a 501(c)(3) that does their charitable and educational work and a 501(c)(4) that does their legislative work. If you want to go in this direction, you'll need a separate board of directors and separate financial record keeping for each organization (although you can share space).

ELECTION-RELATED ACTIVITIES

Regardless of whether your nonprofit chooses the 501(h) election, it's *always* legal for any nonprofit, other than a private foundation, to register people to vote and transport them to the polls as long as you're not bringing them to the polls to vote for a particular candidate. Neither of those activities counts toward a nonprofit's lobby limits, even if you're still operating under the substantial part test. You can do all kinds of simple things like having voter registration forms at your reception desk and at community events and/or providing registration forms for your staff, board, volunteers, and clients. The organization Nonprofit Vote has a ton of resources available on its website (https://www.nonprofitvote.org/nonprofits-voting-elections-online/ voter-registration/), which I encourage you to check out. They'll also help you figure out what to do to be in compliance with the laws of your state.

And even though 501(c)(3)s can't endorse or oppose candidates for public office, there is so much they can do during an election year! In fact, elections provide nonprofits with all kinds of opportunities to engage and forge early relationships with candidates, as long as those activities are nonpartisan. You can:

- **Invite *all* viable candidates to tour your organization or its programs**. This is a terrific way for you to get to know the future officeholder and for having that person know you and your organization. To be clear, you can't cherry pick and invite only those you like—the word *all* is in italics for a reason!
- **Hold candidate forums or debates.** This is especially powerful if your organization has a large grassroots constituency. Imagine the reaction of candidates who come to a community forum and see 500 voters in the audience! That will translate into lobbying power later on.

If you host a debate, there are certain rules that you need to follow. For example, you need to be sure to invite all viable candidates, make sure that your nonprofit doesn't appear to be supporting or opposing anyone in particular (so no trash talking, or trash Tweeting, about anyone before or afterward), and be sure you ask questions that aren't entirely related to what your organization does (so, for example, you might throw in a question or two about your city or region or taxes).

- **Send all viable candidates a questionnaire** and post the results on your website or in your newsletter. There are rules for questionnaires that are similar to the ones for debates. Be sure not to ask yes/no questions, ask a few questions that aren't related to your particular issue, and don't highlight or comment on any candidate responses.

- **Create a voter guide** that is based on your candidate questionnaire.

Remember, for all these activities, it's essential that your organization does not appear in any way to support or oppose any candidate for office! If you do activities like these, you'll ensure that the issues you care about are discussed during an election campaign. In addition, your nonprofit will be associated as being a leader on those issues and be better positioned to push its agenda through the legislative and regulatory processes.

If you've read this chapter and thought "s#@t! our nonprofit has been violating the laws governing nonprofit lobbying and we didn't even know it!!" fear not. First, it is unlikely in the extreme that the IRS will be hot on the trail to audit your organization. After you take a deep breath, be sure to understand the rules, review them with your staff and board, and put in place mechanisms for tracking your time and expenses.

Finally, if you want more information on anything and everything in this appendix, I strongly encourage you to contact the wonderful folks at the Bolder Advocacy initiative at the Alliance for Justice. They have amazing (free) resources and expertise to share. You can find them at Bolderadvocacy.org.

REFERENCE

i. Lu, J. (2018). Organizational antecedents of nonprofit engagement in policy advocacy: A meta-analytical review. *Nonprofit and Voluntary Sector Quarterly*, 47(4_suppl), 177S–203S.

INDEX

AARP, 169
acts, 10
advocacy vs. lobbying, 11–2
Alliance for Justice, 11
   Bolder Advocacy initiative, 171
all-offender laws, 12
Aposhian, Chuck, 93
assembly members, defined, 13
author of a bill, defined, 14

ballot campaigns, 10, 14–5, 74, 161,
   161n5
Benitez, Wayne, 45
bill, use of term, 9, 9n2, 14
bill passage, monitoring progress of
   (Step 10), 20, 141–56
   committee hearings, 143, 145–6,
      147–8, 166
   concurrence votes, 148–9
   conference committees, 149
   DXM case study, 150–2
   floor votes for state bills, 147–8
   governor signature on, 148
   governor veto of, 148–9
   language of bill, 142–3, 148
   listening to objections, 145
   meetings with committee members, 144

monitoring implementation
   of, 153–6
policy staff aides and, 142–3, 145
testimony, 145–6, 166
thank you notes, 144, 145, 147
Black Lives Matter movement, 27, 83
blood alcohol level, 12
Bolderadvocacy.org, 171
brainstorming process, 28, 74, 80–2
brand the issue (Step 4), 73–8
   campaign names, 50, 73–6
   DXM case study, 76–7
   example of, 19
   framing your issue, 74–6
budgets, 24–5

California
   Chelsea's law, 26–7
call to action, 159, 162, 165
campaign names, 73–6
candidate debates, 170
carry a bill, defined, 14
case studies. See DXM case study; New York
   Public Interest Research Group
Chelsea's law, 26–7
citizen activism, 27
climate change frame, 75